Taxidermy Vol.12 Tanning

Outlining the Various methods of Tanning

By Various Authors

British Library Cataloguing-in-Publication Data
A catalogue record for this book is available from the
British Library

Taxidermy

Taxidermy (from the Greek for *arrangement of skin*) is the art of preparing, stuffing, and mounting the skins of animals (especially vertebrates) for display (e.g. as hunting trophies) or for other sources of study. Taxidermy can be done on all vertebrate species of animals, including mammals, birds, fish, reptiles, and amphibians. A person who practices taxidermy is called a taxidermist. Taxidermists may practice professionally for museums or as businesses, catering to hunters and fishermen, or as amateurs, such as hobbyists, hunters, and fishermen. To practice taxidermy, one should be very familiar with anatomy, sculpture, and painting, as well as tanning.

The preservation of animal skins has been practiced for a long time. Embalmed animals have even been found with Egyptian mummies. Although embalming incorporates the use of lifelike poses, it is not technically considered taxidermy though. The earliest methods of preservation of birds for natural history cabinets were published in 1748 by the French Academician Réaumur, and four years later, techniques for mounting were described by M. B. Stollas. By the eighteenth century, almost every town had a tannery business. In the nineteenth century, hunters began bringing their trophies to upholstery shops, where the upholsterers would actually sew up the animal skins and stuff them with rags and cotton. The term 'stuffing' or a 'stuffed animal' evolved from this crude form of taxidermy. Professional taxidermists prefer the term 'mounting' to 'stuffing' however. More sophisticated cotton-wrapped wire bodies supporting sewn-on cured skins soon followed.

In France, Louis Dufresne, taxidermist at the *Muséum National d'Histoire Naturelle* from 1793, popularized arsenical soap (utilising the chemical Arsenic) in an article titled, *Nouveau Dictionnaire D'Histoire Naturelle* (1803–1804). This technique enabled the museum to build the greatest collection of birds in the world. Dufresne's methods spread to England in the early nineteenth century, where updated and non-toxic methods of preservation were developed by some of the leading naturalists of the day, including Rowland Ward and Montague Brown. Ward established one of the earliest taxidermy firms, Rowland Ward Ltd. of Piccadilly. Nevertheless, the art of taxidermy remained relatively undeveloped, and the specimens that were created remained stiff and unconvincing.

The golden age of taxidermy was during the Victorian era, when mounted animals became a popular part of interior design and decor. For the Great Exhibition of 1851 in London, John Hancock, widely considered the father of modern taxidermy, mounted a series of stuffed birds as an exhibit. They generated much interest among the public and scientists alike, who considered them superior to earlier models and were regarded as the first lifelike and artistic specimens on display. A judge remarked that Hancock's exhibit 'will go far towards raising the art of taxidermy to a level with other arts, which have hitherto held higher pretensions.'

In the early twentieth century, taxidermy was taken forward under the leadership of artists such as Carl Akeley, James L. Clark, Coleman Jonas, Fredrick and William Kaempfer, and Leon Pray. These and other taxidermists developed anatomically accurate figures which incorporated every detail in artistically interesting poses, with mounts in realistic settings and poses. This was quite a change from the caricatures popularly offered as hunting trophies. The methods of taxidermy have substantially improved over the last century, heightening quality and lowering toxicity. The animal is first skinned in a process similar to removing the skin from a chicken prior to cooking. This can be accomplished without opening the body cavity, so the taxidermist usually does not see internal organs or blood. Depending on the type of skin, preserving chemicals are applied or the skin is tanned. It is then either mounted on a mannequin made from wood, wool and wire, or a polyurethane form. Clay is used to install glass eyes, which are either bought or cast by the taxidermist themselves.

As an interesting side note, with the success of taxidermy has come the sub-genre of 'rogue taxidermy'; the creation of stuffed animals which do not have real, live counterparts. They can represent impossible hybrids such as the jackalope and the skvader, extinct species, mythical creatures such as dragons, griffins, unicorns or mermaids, or may be entirely of the maker's imagination. When the platypus was first discovered by Europeans in 1798, and a pelt and sketch were sent to the UK, some thought the animal to be a hoax. It was supposed that a taxidermist had sewn a duck's beak onto the body of a beaver-like animal. George Shaw, who produced the first description of the animal in the *Naturalist's Shunga Miscellany* in 1799, even took a pair of scissors to the dried skin to check for stitches. Today, although a niche craft, the art of taxidermy - rogue or otherwise, is still thriving.

Other Works in the Series

Contents

THE EARLY HISTORY OF TAXIDERMY

Taxidermy is the art of preserving the skin, together with the fur, feathers, or scales of animals. The word is derived from the Greek words *taxis*, meaning order, arrangement, or preparation, and *derma*, meaning skin. A skin may be so prepared for use as a specimen for study, as an exhibit in museums and private collections, as an ornament, or article of apparel. Formerly, such mounting of animal skins was called "stuffing" and, in many cases, this was actually what was done (Figure 1). The skin was simply stuffed with straw, excelsior, or other similar material until it looked something like the living animal. Now, however, the stuffing process is entirely obsolete, and great care is taken to model the specimens so they look as lifelike as possible. The old-fashioned "bird-stuffer" has been replaced by the taxidermist, or preparator, and the verb "to stuff," as applied to the art of taxidermy, abandoned. The modern taxidermist mounts, or models a specimen; he does not "stuff" it.

The art of taxidermy as we know it today does not appear to be an ancient one, and is probably not more than 300 years old. This statement, of course, applies only to the mounting of specimens. The curing of skins for use as wearing apparel, rugs, and so forth, was perfected in very early days. Tracing back to the beginnings of taxidermy, one might say that prehistoric man was the first to practice this art by tanning animal skins for use as clothing. The early tribes which inhabited ancient Britain had no other means of covering their bodies and often used the skins of animals as adornments for their persons and in their homes. Our own American Indians preserved the heads of porcupines, foxes, raccoons, loons (Figure 2), and other birds and animals as decorations on clothing and equipment and for use

1

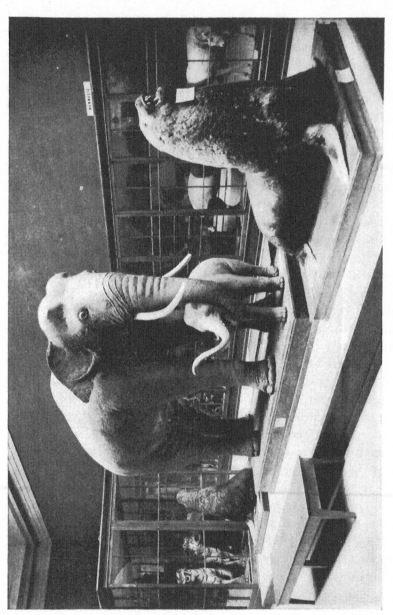

FIGURE 1

2

in ceremonies. The ancient Egyptians also practiced taxidermy of a sort when they embalmed the bodies of dogs, cats, birds, and other animals, although this embalming was accomplished by the use of spices and oils and not by taxidermy methods. Many mummified remains of these birds and animals have been un-

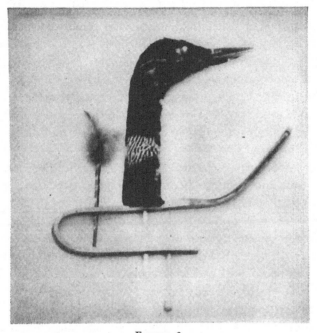

FIGURE 2

earthed in the tombs of Egypt and are on exhibition in museums throughout the world.

The first attempts at taxidermy date back about 350 years. Specimens of birds were collected in India and skinned, and the skins preserved with spices. These were then brought to Holland where they were arranged and held in a somewhat natural position by wires run through the body and anchored to a perch. The oldest specimen of a mounted animal in existence today is a rhinoceros in the Royal Museum of Vertebrates, Florence, Italy,

3

prepared around the year 1600. The methods used in the mounting of this specimen are not known.

That a crude kind of taxidermy was practiced in England toward the end of the eighteenth century is shown by specimens in the Sloane Collection, which in 1753 formed the nucleus of the British Museum in London. At the great exhibitions held in the middle of the nineteenth century throughout Europe, many examples of British taxidermy were exhibited. In America, the Society of American Taxidermists was founded March 24, 1880, but was disbanded three years later, largely because of a lack of cooperation among the taxidermists of the day. This was the first and only organization of its kind in the United States and lasted only long enough to hold three competitive and general exhibitions; the first in Rochester, the second in Boston, and the third in New York City. These exhibitions gave the public a chance to see the art of taxidermy as it was practiced at that time and brought about much higher standards for exhibits by individuals and museums.

For some time, taxidermy had been carried on throughout the world by a small group of men who were more or less secretive and jealous of their methods with the result that many techniques were not widely known. Later, as the need of museums for highly skilled taxidermists became more and more apparent, information came to be circulated more freely. The publication of books and pamphlets on the subject also contributed to breaking down previous secretiveness.

All the early works published on the subject of taxidermy, such as R. A. F. Réaumur's treatise and the *Guides and Instructions* for collecting and preserving natural history specimens, by E. Donovan and others, are now outmoded and only of historical interest to collectors. For field work and the preparation of specimens for scientific purposes, the instructions contained in the publications of museums are of great assistance. The actual mounting of specimens, however, is so intricate and requires such specialized training that it is rarely undertaken successfully by amateurs. A few works have been published dealing with this branch of taxidermy. The reader who wishes to continue taxidermy as a profession will find much that is helpful in John Rowley's *Taxidermy and Museum Exhibition*, published in 1925.

Rowland Ward's, Ltd., the first important taxidermy studio, was founded about 1850 in London, and is still in existence. The work turned out by this studio helped to improve the methods being used in all branches of taxidermy of that time. Associated with the beginnings of taxidermy in America was the Scudder Museum in New York, the collections of which were later acquired by the famous Peale's Museum of the same city. In 1861, Ward's Natural Science Establishment (in no way connected with Rowland Ward's) was founded by Henry A. Ward at Rochester. This famous institution turned out many of the well-known taxidermists and preparators of the time and was a center for the development of the newer methods practiced today. It was at Ward's that the old "stuffing" methods of mounting animals gave way to the modeling and casting techniques considered later in this book. With such leadership, the art of taxidermy has been developed in America to a higher degree than in any other country of the world.

I have used the following method for some years sucessfully on skins up to and including the deer in size. Most larger skins need thinning with a special tool, though an experienced hand can manage to thin a heavy hide with a common draw knife.

An empty lard tub, a half barrel or a large earthenware jar to hold the tan liquor, a fleshing knife and a fleshing beam are necessary to begin with at least. Any smith can make a knife of an old, large file or rasp by working both sides to a blunt edge and drawing the upper end out in a tang for

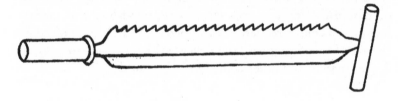

FLESHING KNIFE. (Made from old rasp)

another handle. A piece of old scythe blade with cloth wrapped around the ends will do, or a dull draw knife, either. One blade filed into fine teeth will be useful in removing the inner or muscular skin.

A slab or plank 6 or 7 feet long, with one end tapered and half rounded, on 2 or 4 legs of such length as to bring the end against the workman's chest, makes a beam.

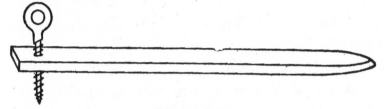

BENCH BEAM.

A short piece of plank rounded off and bolted to the top of the table or work bench will do for small skins.

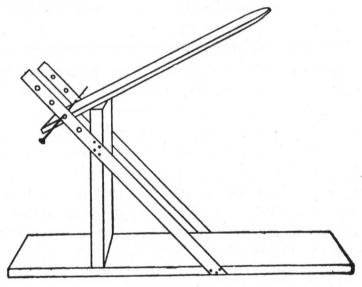

ADJUSTABLE BEAM.

7

Make up the quantity of tanning liquor you wish by the following formula, also given in Chapter III:

Water .... 1 gallon
Salt .... 1 quart

Bring to the boiling point to readily dissolve the salt, and add

Sulphuric acid ...... 1 fluid ounce

Allow it to cool before putting in the skins. *Handle the undiluted acid with care.* Use common coarse salt and the commercial acid. Skins not wanted at once may be left in this pickle for months without injury.

About a gallon of pickle to a fox size skin is the correct amount, but it may be used several times before losing its strength.

After the skin is removed from the carcass any blood and dirt is washed from the fur, the flesh side well salted, rolled up and left 12 to 48 hours. Then thoroughly beam or scrape down the inside of the skin, removing all flesh, fat and muscles. Skins already dry may be placed either in clear water or tan liquor until they soften up. It takes longer to soften in the tan, but if put in water it must be watched or the hair will start, especially in warm weather.

A very hard, dry skin must be soaked and scraped alternately until thoroughly relaxed. When well softened, treat same as a fresh skin. If very fat or greasy, soak the skin in benzine an hour, wring out well, hang up till the benzine is about evaporated, then place in the tan. If not very fat the skin need not be put in the benzine first, but go in the tan at once after being scraped. I use common stove gasoline for benzine; it is as good for the purpose of cleaning and deodorizing, and cheaper. It must never be used in the vicinity of fire or a lighted lamp, as its evaporation produces a very explosive gas. For this reason I do the cleaning and beating of furs out of doors if practicable. Gasoline wrung out of skins may be saved and, after allowing to settle, used again and again. It will not do for the final cleaning of white furs, but for removing grease before tanning, it is as good as any. Stir the skins about in the tan frequently that all parts may come in contact with the solution.

Light skins like the fox will tan in 24 to 48 hours; heavier ones in proportional time. When on pulling or stretching the flesh side, it whitens, it is tanned. On taking from the tan, rinse the skin well in lukewarm water containing a handful of washing soda to the bucketful. Wring out with the hands and soak again in benzine for half an hour. Wring out of this and clean the fur at once as follows:

Fill a shallow box part full of clean sand or

corn meal which has been heated in a pot or pan over the fire or in an oven. Work the skin about in this until the fur is filled with the meal; then shake or beat it out. Repeat the working in meal and beating until the fur is clean and bright. Never put a damp skin into the meal without the gasoline bath first, or you will have the time of your life getting the meal out. Regular fur dressers use very fine saw dust, but meal is to be had anywhere. Plaster of paris will do, but it is most too fine. This treatment with gasoline or benzine removes the grease and animal odors so apt to cling to Indian or home-dressed skins. After cleaning, allow the skin to partly dry in the air and shade; then soften it by stretching, pulling and rubbing in every part. There is no way to accomplish this without work. A pad made of old bags, pieces of blanket, etc., put on the beam, the skin placed on that and stretched in all directions with the blunt edge of the fleshing knife is as good as any way. Keep up the stretching until the skin is quite dry. If any part should dry out too fast for the operator (that is, before it gets stretched) it can be dampened with water on the flesh side and then treated like the rest. If it is wanted extra soft the skin may be thinned down with sandpaper. If the dressed skin is wanted to lie flat as for a rug, it can be moistened on the flesh side; then stretched out and tacked fur side up on a board, the table top or the floor until dry. If this should cause it to harden or stiffen too much break it again without stretching too much.

Another very good tanning solution is the following:

Salt .... 1 quart
Oxalic acid (pulverized).. 4 ounces
Water .... 2 gallons

Dissolve well and immerse the skins, treating them as already directed, rinsing in clear water only. It is also best to allow a little more time for tanning in this solution.

While on the subject of dressing skins a few words in regard to cleaning furs will be in order. White furs especially that have become soiled and matted from use need cleaning frequently and are brought to the furrier or taxidermist for that purpose.

A good washing in gasoline will usually remove the dirt, then dry out as in dressing furs. Furriers often use powdered magnesia for this purpose but almost any finely divided white powder will do about as well. A long siege of beating, shaking and brushing will be necessary to get the drying powder all out of the fur so it will not sift out on the garments when wearing.

If the piece to be cleaned is large (like a coat or cloak) the lining should be removed before cleaning. Neck pieces and small furs are cleaned with linings, wadding, etc., intact. If the fur is so matted that beating does not fluff it out, it must be combed, using a metal fur comb to break up the tangles.

Charges for this work are based on the time used, though at least 75c. or $1.00 each is charged for the small pieces.

As chemicals exposed to the changes of atmosphere are likely to lose strength in time, the owners of mounted heads generally take the precaution of having them poisoned against moth at varying intervals.

Personally I think once in three years is sufficient but some prefer to be on the safe side where valuable heads are concerned and have them treated yearly.

Large heads like buffalo, moose, and elk may be poisoned as they hang, thus obviating any subsequent handling which would be to the detriment of both specimen and operator.

Heads the size of deer and smaller are readily removed and replaced.

First dust the head well and comb the hair or pelt to detect the presence of moth. If loose hairs reveal this the head should be removed to the open air, unscrewed from the shield and saturated with gasoline, which will kill both the moth and its eggs, after which poison against a repetition of the offense.

Pin an old cloth or newspapers about the neck to protect the shield and wall and spray the entire skin of the head with the diluted arsenical solution as recommended in Chapter III. Seedsmen sell a sprayer for use on plants which is about the most convenient size, though the larger size used in the vegetable garden or even a toilet atomizer will distribute the solution.

After it has dried wipe off the eyes and nose with a damp cloth and handle as little as possible.

The common tariff on such work is for treating a single head not less than $1.00. Two to four at one place, 75c. each, and over four, 50c. This for poisoning only. Extra charges for killing moth. Such work should be done in spring or early summer in the Central States in order to be effective.

HOME TANNING OF LEATHER AND SMALL FUR SKINS

By R. W. FREY, *principal chemist,* I. D. CLARKE, *chemist,* and F. P. VEITCH,
*formerly principal chemist in charge, Industrial Farm Products Research Division,
Bureau of Agricultural Chemistry and Engineering* [1]

Contents

THE TANNING of a few hides and skins by inexperienced persons or by those lacking proper equipment is usually inadvisable, from the standpoint both of national economy and of individual profit. Tanners are equipped to make all the leather that the country needs. They can make leather of a better quality and can do it more economically than can the farmer. Under normal conditions, then, farmers and ranchmen should try to improve the quality of the hides and skins that they produce and to market them advantageously, leaving to tanners those trade operations which call for time and equipment and which often result in loss of hides and labor when undertaken by those who have had no experience in the work.

HAVING HIDES TANNED

It may be more economical to have hides and skins tanned by tanners who are willing to tan one or more hides than to do the work on the farm or ranch. Some tanners tan only hides with the hair on for robes or coats; some also tan harness, strap, lace, and glove leather; others tan only harness, strap, or lace leather; and a few tan sole leather. Some accept one-half of the hide in payment for tanning the other half. That is, if a farmer sends a hide to be tanned, the tanner will send back one-half tanned into leather and keep the other half to pay for his work. This probably is the best way for farmers to get their leather.

Depending on the size of the hide, the kind of leather, and the tanner's prices and profits, the charge for tanning a hide with the hair on or making it into leather varies from $1.50 to $4 for calfskins, and from $5 to $8 a hide, or from 25 to 50 cents a square foot or a pound, for horse and cattle hides tanned into harness, lace, or glove leather.

[1] In July 1940 the authors, with the exception of F. P. Veitch (who retired May 31, 1938), and the work on which this publication is based were transferred to the Eastern Regional Research Laboratory, Philadelphia 18, Pa., Bureau of Agricultural and Industrial Chemistry, U. S. Department of Agriculture.

Definite prices can be obtained directly only from a tanner. In writing to tanners be sure to state exactly what kind of hides you have. Give the weight of each, and ask for prices for tanning them with the hair on, making them into robes or coats, or tanning them into the kind of leather you want. The hide you have may not be suitable for the kind of leather you want. It takes a 50-pound or heavier hide to make sole or harness leather. If you tell the tanner what you have, he can tell you what it will make. A list of tanners who tan leather and furs for farmers may be obtained by writing to the Eastern Regional Research Laboratory, Bureau of Agricultural and Industrial Chemistry, Chestnut Hill Station, Philadelphia 18, Pa. In supplying this list of names and addresses the Department assumes no responsibility for the reliability or quality of work of these tanners. The list simply gives the names of all who have informed the Bureau that they will tan one or more hides for farmers.

As a rule, the tanner does not pay shipping charges either way. These, in addition to the tanning charge, must be paid by the farmer.

The regulations for shipping hides by express are now very stringent. Express companies will not accept hides for shipment unless they are packed in a keg or other container that does not leak. Consult the nearest express agent about this before shipping.

Be sure to tag each hide securely before it is shipped with your name and address and the kind of leather you wish made from it. Use a tough linen tag with a reinforced eyelet, and write plainly with indelible pencil. If tag comes off you probably will lose the hide.

BUYING LEATHER BY THE SIDE

Many farmers state that they are offered only 1 to 4 cents a pound for hides but are charged from 90 cents to $1.50 a pound for leather at retail. It may prove more economical in many cases to buy, either individually or cooperatively, leather in quantities larger than a pound or two.

In December 1945, wholesale prices for leather given in trade journals were about as follows: Sole leather crops, 41 to 43 cents a pound; sole leather bends, 43 to 46 cents a pound; sole leather bellies, 25 to 27 cents a pound; single shoulders, 38 to 42 cents, and rough double shoulders, 45 to 48 cents a pound; harness leather sides, 36 to 44 cents a pound, and latigo sides, 35 to 38 cents a square foot; side upper leather, chrome tanned, 26 to 32 cents a square foot. Leather made from packer hides usually sells for more than that made from country hides. Wholesale prices fluctuate from time to time. Definite information on prices at the time of purchase must be obtained from dealers or tanners.

By buying a single side of leather as he needs it, a farmer should be able to get it at a price not more than 10 to 20 percent above wholesale quotations. Expressage on leather bought from tanners must of course, be paid by the purchaser. If whole sides cannot be obtained from dealers in nearby cities or towns at satisfactory prices, write the tanners for their prices.

Sole leather is principally vegetable tanned or chrome tanned and is classed as heavy, medium, and light. For quality it is graded No. 1, No. 2, and No. 3. Chrome sole leather can be bought waxed or unwaxed. Only the waxed is suitable for outdoor use. Harness leather is heavy, medium, and light, and for quality it is graded No. 1 and No. 2, or A and B.

A "side" of leather is half of a tanned hide. It weighs from 15 to 30 pounds, depending upon the size of the hide and the kind of leather. A "back" is a side of leather with the belly, legs, and head trimmed off. Backs cost a little more (3 to 6 cents a pound) than sides. A "bend" is a side of leather with the belly, legs, and shoulder trimmed off. It is the best leather of the hide and is approximately one-half the area or weight of the side. Bends cost more than either backs or sides.

A comparison of the prices at which leather can be bought with the charges for having hides tanned will show which is cheaper. As a general rule, it is believed that it is cheaper to have hides tanned one-half for the other.

HOME TANNING

Sometimes hides and skins can be sold by a farmer or rancher only at prices which are lower than the cost of production. Sometimes "country" hides can scarcely be given away, yet farmers must pay from $1 to $1.50 a pound for leather in small pieces. Under such conditions farmers naturally feel that they must either work up their raw materials or do without the finished leather. As a result, the United States Department of Agriculture has received thousands of requests for directions for farm or home tanning. To meet this demand the following directions have been prepared for tanning one or more hides or skins with only the equipment that can be had on any farm or ranch.

Although good results have been obtained in this Bureau by using the equipment and following the directions here given, inexperienced operators probably often will be unsuccessful. Every attempt, however, will add to their experience and should reduce the number of their failures. Operating on a small scale, they cannot hope to make leather equal in appearance, and possibly in quality, to that on the market. They should, however, be able to make leather which is serviceable for many purposes on farms and ranches.

The directions for tanning need not be memorized, but they must be studied carefully until thoroughly understood before the work is begun. All supplies and equipment should be on hand and all plans should be carefully made before the work is started. It may be necessary to modify the directions, especially those dealing with equipment or tanning conditions. Success in modifying them depends largely upon the individual.

Tanning operations are done best at a uniformly moderate temperature. A cellar, which is naturally fairly warm in winter and cool in summer, is a suitable place. A supply of fresh water near at hand and a drain are convenient.

All the operations can be done in tight, clean wooden barrels, preferably oak, having a capacity of from 40 to 60 gallons. When not in use the barrels should be kept clean and full of water. Half barrels and wooden or fiber buckets are useful for many purposes. Iron containers should never be used. Tools useful in tanning are shown in figure 1.

TANNING HIDES AND SKINS FOR LEATHER

The kind of leather which can be made from a hide or skin depends largely upon the weight and size of the hide or skin. In the tanning trade distinctions in hides and skins are based mainly upon the size and age of the animal and upon the class of leather. Hides from large and adult animals are suitable for sole, harness, belting, or heavy leathers. Skins from small animals, such as sheep, goats, calves, and deer, are made into light and fancy leathers. While there are other commercially important sources of hides and skins, the most important ones are the usual domesticated farm and range animals. As a general rule, the thickness of the finished leather will be about the same as that of the untanned hide. This should be a

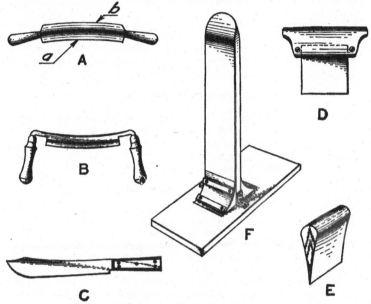

FIGURE 1.—Tools for tanning.

(A) Tanner's fleshing knife, having a blade 15 to 17 inches long: (a) Dull edge for scraping off the hair after liming; (b) very sharp edge for shaving off the flesh.

(B) Eight-inch-blade drawing knife, which may be used instead of A, especially if both handles are bent straight. The back edge may be used for unhairing and the cutting edge for shaving off the flesh.

(C) Twelve-inch-blade butcher knife, which may be used instead of A or B when the point has been driven into a wooden handle or wrapped with leather.

(D) Metal slicker—a dull steel blade about 5 inches square, $\frac{1}{32}$ to $\frac{1}{16}$ inch thick, mounted in a wooden handle.

(E) Wooden slicker, made of hardwood, about 6 inches square, $1\frac{1}{2}$ inches thick at head, shaved down in the shape of a wedge to a thin edge.

(F) Stake for breaking up and softening skins and leather. A board about 3 feet long, 6 inches wide, and 1 inch thick is braced in an upright position to a heavy base or to the floor. The top of the board is rounded and thinned in the shape of a wedge to an edge about $\frac{1}{8}$ inch thick.

guide in selecting skins for different kinds of leather. The first essential for a satisfactory yield of good leather is a sound, clean hide or skin. Skinning should be done properly, without cutting or scoring the hide, and at the same time all of the fat and flesh should be removed; for, if left on, they increase the tendency of the hide to rot or spoil. Farmers' Bulletin 1055, Country Hides and Skins: Skinning, Curing, and Marketing, should be studied in this connection.

Preparation of the hide or skin for tanning may be begun as soon as it has been taken off the animal, drained, and cooled from the body heat. Overnight will be long enough. If tanning is not to be started at once or if there are more hides than can be handled at one time, the hides may be thoroughly salted, using about 1 pound of clean salt for each pound of hide, and kept for from 3 to 5 months. The hides must never be allowed to freeze or heat during storage or tanning. Some tanners state that salting before tanning is helpful. It can do no harm to salt a hide for a few days before it is prepared for tanning.

The directions here given have been prepared for a single heavy cow, steer, or bull hide weighing from 40 to 70 pounds or for an equivalent weight in smaller skins, such as calf or kip skins. The heavy hides are best suited for sole, harness, or belting leather. Lighter hides weighing from 20 to 40 pounds should be used for lace leather.

PRELIMINARY OPERATIONS

Before it is tanned a hide or skin must be put through the following preliminary operations, which are the same for all the leather-making processes given in this bulletin. As soon as the hide or skin has been put through these processes, start the tanning, following the directions given for the particular kind of leather desired.

Slaking Lime

Put from 6 to 8 pounds of burnt or caustic lime in a clean half barrel, wooden tub, or bucket, with a capacity of at least 5 gallons. Use only good-quality lime, free from dirt and stones; never use air-slaked lime. To the lime add about 1 quart of water. As the lime begins to slake add more water, a little at a time, to keep the lime moist. Do not pour in enough water to quench the slaking. When the lime appears to be slaked, stir in 2 gallons of clean water. Do all this just as in making whitewash. Slake the lime on the day before the soaking of the hide is begun and keep the limewater covered with boards or sacks until ready to use it.

If available, fresh hydrated lime, not air-slaked, may be used instead of the burnt or caustic lime. In this case use from 8 to 10 pounds in 4 or 5 gallons of water.

Soaking and Cleaning

If the hide has been salted, shake it vigorously to remove most of the salt. Spread it out, hair side down, and trim off the tail, head, ears, all ragged edges, and shanks.

Place the hide, hair side up, lengthwise, over a smooth log or board, and with a sharp knife split it from neck to tail, straight down the backbone line, into two half hides, or "sides." It will be more convenient in the later handling, especially when the hide is large, to then split each side lengthwise through the "break," just above the flanks, into two strips, making the strip with the backbone edge about twice as wide as the belly strip. Thus a whole hide will give two sides or four strips. If desired, small skins need not be split. In these directions "side" means side, strip, or skin, as the case may be.

Fill a 50-gallon barrel with clean, cool water. Place the sides, flesh side out, over short sticks or pieces of rope and hang them in the barrel of water. Let them soak for 2 or 3 hours. Stir them about frequently to soften, loosen, and wash out the blood, dirt, manure, and salt. The sticks or pieces of rope may be held in place by tying a loop of cord on each end and catching the loops over nails in the outside of the barrel near the top.

After they have soaked for about 3 hours take out the sides, one at a time, and place them, hair side up, over a "beam." A ready-made beam can be bought. A fairly saitsfactory one may be made from a very smooth slab, log, or thick planed board, from 1 to 2 feet wide and

FIGURE 2.—Putting a side into limewater. The hide has been split into two sides and soaked and cleaned. Each side is folded over a stick.

6 to 8 feet long. The slab or log is inclined, with one end resting on the ground and the other extending over a box or trestle so as to be about waist high. With the side lying hair side up over the beam, scrub off all dirt and manure, using if necessary a stiff brush. Wash off with several bucketfuls of clean water.

Turn the side over, flesh side up, and scrape or cut off any remaining flesh. Work over the entire flesh side with the back edge of a drawing or butcher knife held firmly against the hide, pushing away from the body. Wash off with one or two bucketfuls of clean water. This working over should always be done.

19

Refill the soak barrel with clean, cool water and hang the sides in it as before. Pull them up and stir them about frequently until they are soft and flexible. Usually a green or fresh hide needs to be soaked for not more than from 12 to 24 hours and a green salted hide for not more than from 24 to 48 hours.

When the sides are properly softened—that is, when they are about like a fresh hide or skin—throw them over the beam and thoroughly scrape off all remaining flesh and fat. It is of the greatest importance to remove all this material. When it cannot be scraped off, cut it off, but be careful not to cut into the hide itself. Even should there appear to be no flesh to take off and nothing seems to be removed,

FIGURE 3 — Ready to unhair after liming. When the hair can be rubbed off easily with the hand the hide is ready to be unhaired.

it is necessary to thoroughly work over the flesh side in this way with the back of a knife. Finally wash it off with a bucketful of clean water.

The side must be soft, pliable, and clean all over before being put into the lime, which is the next step.

Liming

Wash out the soak barrel, pour in all of the slaked lime, nearly fill the barrel with clean, cool water, and stir thoroughly. Again place the sides, hair side out, over the short sticks or pieces of rope, and hang them in the barrel so that they are completely covered by the limewater (fig. 2). See that the sides have as few folds or wrinkles as possible, and also be sure that no air is trapped under them. Keep the barrel covered with boards or bags. Pull up the sides and stir the limewater three or four times each day until the hair will come off easily. This takes from 6 to 10 days in summer and possibly as many as 16 days in winter.

When thoroughly limed, the hair can be rubbed off readily with the hand (fig. 3). Early in the liming process it will be possible to pull out the hair, but the hide must be left in the limewater until the hair comes off by rubbing over with the hand. For harness and

FIGURE 4.—Unhairing. After thorough liming, the hair is pushed or scraped off with a dull metal edge. At the same time some of the lime, grease, and dirt are worked out of the hide. Here the workman is using the dull edge of the fleshing knife and a tanner's beam.

belting leathers leave the hide in the limewater for from 3 to 5 days after this condition has been reached

Unhairing

After the side has been limed, throw it hair side up, over the beam and with the back edge of a drawing or butcher knife held nearly flat against the side push off the hair from all parts (fig. 4). If the side is sufficiently limed, a curdy or cheesy layer of skin rubs off with the hair. If this layer does not rub off, the side must be returned to the limewater. Now thoroughly work over the grain or hair side with a dull-edged tool to "scud" or work out as much lime, grease, and dirt as possible.

21

Turn the side over and scud it again, being sure to remove all fleshy matter. Shave down to the hide itself, but be careful not to cut into it. Remove the flesh by scraping and by using a very sharp knife (fig. 1), with a motion like that of shaving the face (fig. 5).

Now proceed as directed under Bark-Tanned Sole and Harness Leather (p. 9), Chrome-Tanned Leather (p. 13), or Alum-Tanned Lace Leather (p. 18), depending upon the kind of leather desired.

FIGURE 5.—Fleshing. All flesh, fat, and tissue must be shaved off down to the real hide or skin.

Wastes from Liming

The lime, limewater, sludge, and fleshings from the liming process may be used as fertilizer, particularly for acid soils. The hair, as it is scraped from the hide, may be collected separately and after being rinsed several times may be used in plastering. If desired, it can be thoroughly washed with many changes of water until absolutely clean and after being dried out in a warm place used for padding, upholstering, insulation of pipes, etc.

BARK-TANNED SOLE AND HARNESS LEATHER

Deliming

After the sides have been put through the unhairing and fleshing operations, rinse them with clean water. Wash the sides in cool, clean water for from 6 to 8 hours, changing the water frequently.

Buy 5 ounces of U. S. P. (United States Pharmacopœia) lactic acid (or 16 ounces of tannery 22 percent lactic acid). Nearly fill a clean 40- to 50-gallon barrel with clean, cool water, stir in the lactic acid, and mix the water and acid thoroughly with a paddle. Hang the sides in the barrel and leave them there for 24 hours, pulling them up and stirring them frequently.

Take out the sides, work over or scud them thoroughly, as directed under Unhairing (p. 8), and hang them in a barrel of cold water.

FIGURE 6.—Unhaired, fleshed hide ready to be delimed. All hair, flesh, and fat must be removed, as well as much of the lime and grease.

Change the water several times, and finally leave them in the water overnight.

If lactic acid cannot be obtained, use a gallon of vinegar instead.

Tanning

The sides are now ready for the actual tanning. From 15 to 20 days before this stage will be reached, weigh out from 30 to 40 pounds of good quality, finely ground oak or hemlock bark and pour onto it about 20 gallons of boiling water.

Finely ground bark, with no particles larger than a grain of corn, will give the best results. Simply chopping the bark into coarse pieces will not do. Do not let the tan liquor come in contact with iron vessels. Use the purest water available. Rain water is best.

Let this bark infusion stand in a covered vessel until ready to use it. Stir it occasionally. When ready to start tanning, strain off the bark liquor through a clean, coarse sack into the tanning barrel. Fill the barrel about three-quarters full with water, rinsing the bark with this water so as to get out as much tannin as possible. Add 2 quarts of vinegar. Stir well. Place the sides, from the deliming, over sticks, and hang them in this bark liquor with as few folds and wrinkles as possible. Move the sides about and change their position often in order to get an even color.

Just as soon as the sides have been hung in the bark liquor, again soak from 30 to 40 pounds of ground bark in about 20 gallons of hot water. Let this second bark liquor stand until the sides have become evenly colored, or for from 10 to 15 days. Take out of the tanning barrel 5 gallons of liquor and pour in about one-quarter of the second bark liquor. Also add about 2 quarts more of vinegar and stir it in well. Five days later take out a second 5 gallons of tanning liquor from the barrel and add another fourth of the tan liquor only (no vinegar). Do this every 5 days until the second bark liquor is used up.

The progress of the tanning varies somewhat with conditions and can best be followed by inspecting a small sliver cut from the edge of the hide. About 35 days after the actual tanning has been started a fresh cut should show two dark or brown narrow streaks about as wide as a heavy pencil line coming in from each surface of the hide.

At this stage weigh out about 40 pounds of fine bark and just moisten it with hot water. Do not add more water than the bark will soak up. Pull the sides out of the bark liquor and dump in the moistened bark, keeping in the barrel as much of the old tan liquor as possible. Mix thoroughly and while mixing hang the sides back in the barrel. Actually bury them in the bark. All parts of the sides must be kept well down in the bark mixture. Leave the sides in this bark for about 6 weeks and move them about once in a while.

At the end of 6 weeks pull the sides out. A cutting should show that the tanning has spread nearer to the center. Pour out about half the liquor. Stir the bark in the barrel, hang the sides back, and fill the barrel with fresh, finely ground bark. Leave the sides in for about 2 months, shaking the barrel from time to time and adding bark and water as needed to keep the sides completely covered.

At the end of this time the hide should be evenly colored all the way through, without any white or raw streak in the center of a cut edge. If it is not struck through, it must be left longer in the wet bark, and more bark may be needed.

For harness, strap, and belting leather the sides may be taken out of the bark liquor at this stage, but for sole leather they must be left for 2 months longer. When fully tanned through, the sides are ready for oiling and finishing.

Oiling and Finishing

HARNESS AND BELTING LEATHER.—Take the sides from the tan liquor, rinse them off with water, and scour the grain or hair side thoroughly with plenty of warm water and a stiff brush. Then go over the sides with a "slicker" (fig. 1), pressing the slicker firmly against

24

the leather while pushing it away from the body and work out as much water as possible. "Slick" out on the grain or hair side in all directions (fig. 7). For harness, belting, and the like this scouring and slicking must be done thoroughly.

A slicker can be made from a piece of copper or brass about one-fourth inch thick, 6 inches long, and 4 inches wide. One long edge of the slicker is mounted in a wooden handle and the other long edge is finished smooth and well rounded. A piece of hardwood, about 6 inches square, 1½ inches thick at the head, and shaved down wedge-shape to a thin edge will also serve as a slicker (fig. 1).

FIGURE 7.—Slicking out. After tanning and after greasing, the leather should be worked out on both sides with a slicker.

While the sides are still damp, but not very wet, go over the grain or hair side with a liberal coating of neat's-foot or cod oil. Hang up the sides and let them dry out slowly. When dry, take them down and dampen well by dipping in water or by rolling them up in wet sacking or burlap.

When uniformly damp and limber, evenly brush or mop over the grain or hair side a thick coating of warm dubbin. The dubbin is made by melting together about equal parts of cod oil and tallow or neat's-foot oil and tallow. This dubbin when cool must be soft and pasty, but not liquid.

Hang up the sides again and leave until thoroughly dry. When dry, scrape off the excess tallow by working over with the slicker. If more grease in the leather is desired, dampen again and apply another coating of the dubbin, giving a light application to the flesh

25

side also. When again dry, remove the tallow and thoroughly work over all parts of the leather with the slicker. Rubbing over with sawdust will help to take up any surface oiliness.

If it is desired to blacken the leather, this must be done before greasing. A black dye solution can be made by dissolving one-half ounce of water-soluble nigrosine in 1¼ pints of water, with the addition, if handy, of several drops of ammonia. Evenly mop or brush this solution over the dampened but ungreased leather and then grease as directed in the preceding paragraph.

SOLE LEATHER.—Take the sides from the tan liquor and rinse them thoroughly with clean water. Hang them up until they are only damp and then apply a good coating of neat's-foot or cod oil to the grain or hair side. Again hang them up until they are thoroughly dry.

When repairing shoes with this leather it is advisable, after cutting out the piece for soling, to dampen and hammer it down well, and then, after putting it on the shoe, to make it waterproof and more serviceable by setting the shoe in a shallow pan of melted grease or oil and letting it stand for about 15 minutes. The grease or oil must be no hotter than the hand can bear. Rubber heels should not be put in oil or grease. The soles of shoes with rubber heels may be waterproofed in the same way, using a piepan for the oil or grease and placing the heels outside the pan. Any good oil or grease will do. The following formulas have been found satisfactory:

	Ounces
Formula 1:	
Neutral wool grease	8
Dark petrolatum	4
Paraffin wax	4
Formula 2:	
Petrolatum	16
Beeswax	2
Formula 3:	
Petrolatum	8
Paraffin wax	4
Wool grease	4
Crude turpentine gum (gum thus)	2
Formula 4:	
Tallow	12
Cod oil	4

CHROME-TANNED LEATHER

For many purposes chrome-tanned leather is considered to be as good as the more generally known bark or vegetable-tanned leather. The chrome process, which takes only a few weeks as against as many months for the bark-tanning process, derives its name from the use of chemicals containing chromium or "chrome." It is a chemical process requiring great care. It is felt, however, that by following exactly the directions here given, never disregarding details which may seem unimportant, a serviceable leather can be produced in a comparatively short time. The saving in time seems sufficient to justify a trial of this process.

Deliming

After the sides have been put through the unhairing and fleshing operations (pp. 8 and 9) rinse them off with clean water.

26

If sole, belting, or harness leather is to be tanned, soak and wash the sides in cool water for about 6 hours before putting them into the lactic acid. Change the water four or five times.

If strap, upper, or thin leather is to be tanned, put the limed white sides into a wooden or fiber tub of clean, lukewarm (about 90° F.) water and let them stay there for from 4 to 8 hours before putting them into the lactic acid. Stir the sides about occasionally. Be sure that the water is not too hot. It never should be so hot that it is uncomfortably warm to the hand.

For each large hide or skin buy 5 ounces of U. S. P. lactic acid (or 16 ounces of tannery 22 percent lactic acid). Nearly fill a clean 40- to 50-gallon barrel with clean, cool water, and stir in the lactic acid, mixing thoroughly with a paddle. Hang the sides in the barrel, and leave them there for 24 hours, plunging them up and down occasionally.

For light skins, weighing less than 15 pounds, use only 2 ounces of U. S. P. lactic acid in about 20 gallons of water.

If lactic acid cannot be obtained, use 1 pint of vinegar for every ounce of lactic acid. An effort should be made to get the lactic acid, however, for vinegar will not be as satisfactory, especially for the medium and smaller skins.

After deliming, work over both sides of the side as directed under Unhairing (p. 8).

For sole, belting, and harness leathers, hang the sides in a barrel of cool water overnight. Then proceed as directed under Tanning.

For thin, softer leathers from small skins, do not soak the sides in water overnight. Simply rinse them off with water and proceed as directed under Tanning.

Tanning

The tanning solution should be made up at least 2 days before it is to be used—that is, not later than when the sides are taken from the limewater for the last time.

Remember that this is a chemical process and that all materials must be of good quality and accurately weighed and the specified quantities of water carefully measured.

The following chemicals are required: Chrome alum (chromium potassium sulfate crystals); soda crystals (crystallized sodium carbonate); and common salt (sodium chloride). Insist upon pure chemicals of the United States Pharmacopœia quality. Get them from the nearest drugstore or find out from it the address of a chemical manufacturing concern which can supply them.

For each hide or skin weighing more than 30 pounds use the following quantities for the stock chrome solution:

Dissolve 3½ pounds of soda crystals (crystallized sodium carbonate) and 6 pounds of common salt (sodium chloride) in 3 gallons of warm, clean water in a wooden or fiber bucket. The soda crystals must be clear or glasslike. Do not use the white crusted lumps.

At the same time dissolve in a large tub or half barrel 12 pounds of chrome alum (chromium potassium sulfate crystals) in 9 gallons of cool, clean water. This will take some time to dissolve and will need frequent stirring. Here again it is important to use only the very dark, hard, glossy, purple or plum-colored crystals of chrome alum, not the lighter, crumbly, dull-lavender ones.

When the chemicals are dissolved, which can be told by feeling around in the tubs with a paddle, pour the soda-salt solution slowly in a thin stream into the chrome-alum solution, stirring constantly. Take at least 10 minutes to pour in the soda solution. This should give one solution of about 12 gallons, which is the stock chrome solution. Keep this solution well covered in a wooden or fiber bucket, tub, or half barrel.

To start tanning, pour one-third (4 gallons) of the stock chrome solution into a clean 50-gallon barrel and add about 30 gallons of clean, cool water; that is, fill the barrel about two-thirds full. Thoroughly mix the solution in the barrel and hang in it the sides from the deliming. Work the sides about and stir the solution frequently, especially during the first 2 or 3 days. This helps to give the sides an even color. It should be done every hour or so throughout the first day. Keep the sides as smooth as possible.

After 3 days, temporarily remove the sides from the barrel. Add one-half of the remaining stock chrome solution, thoroughly mixing it with that in the barrel, and again hang in the sides. Move the sides about and stir the solution 3 or 4 times each day.

Three days later, once more temporarily remove the sides. Pour into the barrel the rest of the stock chrome solution, thoroughly mixing it with that in the barrel, and again hang in the sides. Move the sides about and stir frequently as before.

After the sides have been in this solution for 3 or 4 days, cut off a small piece of the thickest part of the side, usually in the neck, and examine the freshly cut edge of the piece. If the cut edge seems to be evenly colored greenish or bluish all the way through, the tanning is about finished. Boil the small piece in water for a few minutes. If it curls up and becomes hard or rubbery, the tanning is not completed and the sides must be left in the tanning solution for a few days longer, or until a small piece when boiled in water is changed little if at all.

The foregoing quantities and directions have been given for a medium or large hide. For smaller hides and skins the quantities of chemicals and water can be reduced. For each hide or skin weighing less than 30 pounds, or for two or three small skins together weighing not more than 30 pounds, the quantities of chemicals may be cut in half, giving the following solutions:

For the soda-salt solution, dissolve 1¾ pounds of soda crystals (crystallized sodium carbonate) and 3 pounds of common salt (sodium chloride) in 1½ gallons of clean water.

For the chrome-alum solution, dissolve 6 pounds of chrome alum (chromium potassium sulfate crystals) in 4½ gallons of cool, clean water.

When the chemicals are dissolved pour the soda-salt solution slowly into the chrome-alum solution as already described. This will give one solution of about 6 gallons which is the stock chrome solution. For the lighter skins tan with this solution, exactly as directed for medium and large hides, adding one-third, that is, 2 gallons, of this stock chrome solution each time, and begin to tan in about 15 gallons instead of 30 gallons of water. Follow the directions already given as to stirring, number of days, and testing to determine when tanning is completed. Very small, thin skins probably will not take as long to tan as will the large hides. The boiling-water test is very reliable for showing when the hide is tanned.

When the sides are tanned, take them out of the tanning solution and put them in a barrel of clean water. The barrel in which the tanning was done can be used after it has been thoroughly washed.

When emptying the tanning barrel be sure carefully to dispose of the tanning solution. Although not poisonous to the touch, it probably would be fatal to farm animals should they drink it, and it is harmful to soil.

Wash the sides in about four changes of water. For medium and large hides, dissolve 2 pounds of borax in about 40 gallons of clean water and soak the sides in this solution overnight. For hides and skins weighing less than 25 pounds, use 1 pound of borax in about 20 gallons of water. Move the sides about in the borax solution as often as feasible. After soaking overnight in the borax solution, remove the sides and wash them for an entire day, changing the water five or six times. Take the sides out, let the water drain off, and proceed as directed under Dyeing Black, or, if it is not desired to blacken the leather, proceed as directed under Oiling and Finishing.

Dyeing Black

WATER-SOLUBLE NIGROSINE.—One of the simplest and best means of dyeing leather black is to use nigrosine. Make up the dye solution in the proportion of one-half ounce of water-soluble nigrosine dissolved in 1¼ pints of water. Be sure to get water-soluble nigrosine. Evenly mop or brush this solution over the damp leather after draining as already directed and then proceed as directed under Oiling and Finishing.

IRON LIQUOR AND SUMAC.—If water-soluble nigrosine cannot be obtained, a fairly good black may be secured with iron liquor and sumac. To make the iron liquor, mix clean iron filings or turnings with one-half gallon of good vinegar and let the mixture stand for several days. See that there are always some undissolved filings or turnings in the vinegar. For a medium or large hide put from 10 to 15 pounds of dried crumbled sumac leaves in a barrel containing from 35 to 40 gallons of warm water. Stir well and when cool hang in it the wet, chrome-tanned sides. Leave the sides in this solution for about 2 days, pulling them up and mixing the solution frequently. Take out the sides, rinse off all bits of sumac, and evenly mop or brush over with the iron liquor. Rinse off the excess of iron liquor and put the sides back in the sumac overnight. If not black enough the next morning, mop over again with iron liquor, rinse, and return to the sumac solution for a day. Take the sides out of the sumac, rinse well, and scrub thoroughly with warm water. Finally wash the sides for a few hours in several changes of water.

While both of these formulas for dyeing have been given, it is recommended that water-soluble nigrosine be used whenever possible, as the iron liquor and sumac formula is somewhat troublesome and may produce a cracky grain. After blackening, proceed as directed under Oiling and Finishing.

Oiling and Finishing

THIN LEATHER.—Let the wet tanned leather from the dyeing, or, if not dyed, from the neutralizing, dry out slowly. While it is still very damp go over the grain or hair side with a liberal coating of neat's-foot or cod oil. While still damp, tack the sides out on a wall or tie them in frames (shown on cover), being sure to pull them out tight and smooth, and leave them until dry. When dry take down and dampen well by dipping in warm water or by rolling them up in wet sacking or burlap. When uniformly damp and limber go over the sides with a "slicker" (fig. 1), pressing the slicker firmly against

FIGURE 8.—Staking. To soften leather and tanned skins, work them repeatedly back and forth in all directions over a dull edge. This must be done when the leather is drying.

the leather, while pushing it away from the body. Slick out on the grain or hair side in all directions (fig. 7).

After slicking it may be necessary to "stake" the leather (fig. 8). This is done by pulling the damp leather vigorously back and forth over the edge of a small smooth board about 3 feet long, 6 inches wide, and 1 inch thick, fastened upright and braced to the floor or ground. The top end of the board must be shaved down to a wedge shape, with the edge not more than one-eighth-inch thick and the corners well-rounded (fig. 1). Pull the sides, flesh side down, backward and forward over this edge, exactly as a cloth is worked back and forth in polishing shoes.

30

Let the sides dry out thoroughly again. If not sufficiently soft and pliable, dampen them with water, apply more oil, and slick and stake as before. The more time given to slicking and staking, the smoother and more pliable the leather will be.

THICK LEATHER.—Thick leather from the larger hides is oiled and finished in a slightly different manner. For harness and strap leather, let the tanned sides, dyed if desired, dry down. While they are still quite damp slick over the grain or hair side thoroughly and apply a liberal coating of neat's-foot or cod oil. Tack on a wall or tie in a frame, stretching the leather out tight and smooth, and leave until dry. Take the sides down, dampen them with warm water until limber and pliable, and apply to the grain side a thick coating of warm dubbin. The dubbin is made by melting together about equal parts of cod oil and tallow or neat's-foot oil and tallow. When cool it must be soft and pasty but not liquid. If too nearly liquid, add more tallow. Hang up the sides again and leave them until thoroughly dried. When dry, scrape off the excess tallow by working over with the slicker. If more grease in the leather is desired, dampen again and apply another coating of the dubbin. When again dry, slick off the tallow and thoroughly work over all parts of the leather with the slicker. Rubbing over with sawdust helps to take up surface oiliness.

Chrome-tanned leather is stretchy, so that in cutting the leather for use in harness, straps, reins, and similar articles it is best to first take out most of the stretch.

Chrome leather for shoe soles must be heavily greased, or, in other words, waterproofed, unless it is to be worn in extremely dry regions. Waterproofing may be done after repairing the shoes by setting them in a shallow pan of oil or grease so that just the soles are covered by the grease. The soles should be dry before they are set in the melted grease. Melted paraffin wax will do, although it makes the soles stiff. The simple formulas given on page 13 are satisfactory for waterproofing chrome sole leather.

ALUM-TANNED LACE LEATHER

Deliming

After the sides have been put through the unhairing and fleshing operations (pp. 8 and 9), rinse them off with cool, clean water for from 6 to 8 hours, changing the water frequently.

Buy 5 ounces of U. S. P. lactic acid (or 16 ounces of tannery 22 percent lactic acid). Nearly fill a clean 40- to 50-gallon barrel with clean, cool water and stir in the lactic acid, mixing throughly with a paddle. Hang the sides in the barrel and leave them there for 24 hours, pulling them up and stirring them about frequently. Take out the sides, work over or scud thoroughly, as directed under Unhairing (p. 8), and hang them in a barrel of cool water. Change the water several times, and finally leave them in the water overnight. If lactic acid cannot be obtained, use a gallon of vinegar instead.

Tanning

While the sides are being delimed, thoroughly wash out the barrel in which the hide was limed. Put in it 15 gallons of clean water and 12 pounds of ammonia alum or potash alum and stir frequently until it is completely dissolved.

31

Dissolve 3 pounds of washing soda (crystallized sodium carbonate) and 6 pounds of salt in 5 gallons of cold, clean water in a wooden bucket. The soda crystals must be clear and glasslike. Do not use white crusted lumps.

Pour the soda solution into the alum solution in the barrel very, very slowly, stirring the solution in the barrel constantly. Take at least 10 minutes to pour in the soda solution in a small stream. If the soda is poured in rapidly the solution will become milky and will not tan. The solution should be cool, and enough water to nearly fill the barrel should be added.

Hang each well-washed side from the deliming in the alum-soda solution. Pull up the sides and stir the solution six or eight times each day. Do not put the bare hands in the liquor if they are cut or cracked or have sores on them.

After 6 or 7 days remove the sides from the alum-soda solution and rinse well for about a quarter of an hour in clean, cold water.

Oiling and Finishing

Let the sides drain and dry out slowly. While still very damp go over the grain or hair side with a liberal coating of neat's-foot or cod oil. After the oil has gone in and the sides have dried a little more but are still slightly damp, begin to work them over a "stake." The time to start staking is important. The sides must not be too damp; neither must they be too dry. When light spots or light streaks appear on folding it is time to begin staking. Alum-tanned leather must be thoroughly and frequently staked.

Staking is done by pulling the damp leather vigorously back and forth over the edge of a small, smooth board (fig. 1), as described on page 17. The sides must be staked thoroughly all over in order to make them pliable and soft, and the staking must be continued at intervals until the leather is dry.

When dry, evenly dampen the sides by dipping them in water or by leaving them overnight covered with wet burlap or sacks. Apply to the grain or hair side a thick coating of warm dubbin. The dubbin is made by melting together about equal parts of neat's-foot oil and tallow or cod oil and tallow. When cool, the dubbin must be soft and pasty but not liquid. If too nearly liquid, add more tallow. Leave the greased sides, preferably in a warm place, until dry. Scrape off the excess tallow and again stake the sides. If the leather is too hard and stiff, dampen it evenly with water before staking.

After staking, go over the sides with a slicker (fig. 1), pressing the slicker firmly against the leather, while pushing it away from the body. Slick out on the grain, or hair side, in all directions (fig. 7).

Alum-tanned leather almost invariably dries out the first time hard and stiff. It must be dampened again and restaked while drying. In some cases this must be done repeatedly, and another application of dubbin may be necessary. By repeated dampening, staking, and slicking the leather can be made as soft and pliable as desired.

TANNING FUR SKINS

Much of the value of a fur skin depends upon the manner in which it is handled in the raw state. After the animal has been caught, every effort should be made to follow the best practices in skinning and curing, in order to obtain a skin of the greatest possible value. Certain trade customs also must be followed to secure the top price. Detailed information on the manner of skinning and curing skins from the better known fur-bearing animals is given in United States Department of Agriculture Yearbook Separate 823. Trapping on the Farm, part of the 1919 Yearbook.

Requests for directions for tanning fur skins are constantly received by the Department of Agriculture. There is, however, less need for such information than there is for information on farm or

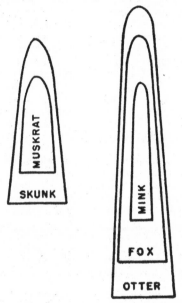

FIGURE 9.—Stretching boards for fur skins. Cased fur skins are dried on boards of different sizes and shapes, depending upon the kind of skin.

home tanning of hides and skins into leather. Fur skins as a protection are a necessity for those living in cold climates, but comparatively few are used for this purpose. Most of the fur skins are made into articles which are more or less of a luxury and, as such, are valued largely on the basis of their appearance and finish, which an inexperienced worker can seldom make sufficiently pleasing. Furthermore, raw fur skins are valuable, and, if well cared for, usually find a ready market. Nevertheless, the spread between the prices paid for raw furs and those demanded for finished fur articles is enormous. No doubt, this spread in many instances inspires the attempts at home manufacture.

An inexperienced person should not try to tan valuable fur skins or large hides, such as cattle, horse, or bear, for making into coats, robes, or rugs. The risk of damage or of an unsatisfactory product, as measured by the usual standards of finish and appearance, is too great. The difficulties in properly handling large hides make the

33

chances of success remote, except by those having suitable equipment and experience. Moreover, tanning the skin is only one step in the production of the finished article. After being tanned, all skins must be tailored, many must be dyed, and small ones must be matched, blended, and sewed together. All these operations require experience and practice to secure the attractive appearance desired by wearers of furs. Some of the operations, such as those of bleaching and dyeing, are so highly specialized that their undertaking should not even be considered by an amateur. From the standpoint of serviceability and usefulness, inexperienced persons might meet with a fair degree of success in tanning and tailoring fur skins, but few can ever hope to make a fur piece or garment which will compare favorably in appearance with the shop or factory product. The tanning and dressing of fur skins, then, are best left to those who are experienced and equipped to carry out the tedious operations required.

To satisfy the demand upon the Department for information on the home tanning of fur skins and to provide those who insist upon carrying on such work with correct information and with detailed methods which offer the best chances for success, the following directions are given. These directions are meant primarily for small fur skins no larger than that of the fox and for skins of low market value.

No formulas for tanning are foolproof, and success can be attained only by close observation, plenty of work, and the exercise of care and patience. All skins are not treated just alike. In fact, each skin has its own peculiarities, which only experience can show how to treat. Some skins are tough and fairly thick and will stand mistreatment; others are very thin and tender and are easily ruined. Some are fat and greasy and require thorough working out of the grease; others do not. An inexperienced person should experiment with the least valuable skins. If a number of skins of the same kind are to be tanned, one or two of the poorest should be tried first.

SOAKING AND FLESHING

The first step is to get the skin thoroughly softened, cleaned, and free from flesh and grease.

Split the tail the entire length on the underside. If the skin is "cased," split it neatly down the middle of the belly. Soak it in several changes of clear, cool water. When the skin begins to soften, lay it on a beam or smooth pole and begin working over the flesh side to break up the adhering tissue and fat. All dried skins have a shiny, tight layer of tissue. This tissue must be broken up and entirely removed, which is best done by repeated alternate working and soaking. A good tool for scratching the tissue is a metal edge of any kind, such as a drawing knife or an ordinary knife with dull saw teeth or notches filed in it. Working over with these dull teeth scratches or breaks up the tissue so that it can be scraped off after further soaking.

At the same time the grease and oil are worked out of the skin. This operation is of the utmost importance. It is utterly useless to start tanning until all the tissue and grease have been removed and the skin is uniformly soft and pliable, without any hard spots.

The time of soaking depends upon the condition of the skin. Some skins require only about 2 hours, while others need a much longer

34

time. Very hard skins often must be thoroughly dampened, rolled up, fur side out, and put away in a cool place overnight to soften. While a skin must be soaked until soft, it should not stay wet longer than necessary, as the hair may start to slip.

In fleshing and scraping, care also must be taken not to injure the true skin or expose the hair roots, especially on thin skins.

When the soaking is well advanced and the skin is getting in good shape, work it in lukewarm water containing an ounce of soda or borax to the gallon. Soap also may be added. This treatment promotes softening, cleans the skin, and cuts the grease.

Work again over the beam and finally rinse thoroughly in lukewarm water. Squeeze out most of the water, but do not wring the skin. Without further drying, work the skin in gasoline, using several changes if very much dirt and grease are present. Squeeze and hang up the skin for a few minutes.

The skin should now be ready for tanning. When painting or pasting of the tan liquor on the flesh side only is included in the directions for tanning, it is best to dry out the hair or fur side first by working in sawdust. In this way any heating of the fur side while the skin is tacked out is avoided, as are also matting and stiffening of the fur. If while drying out the fur, the flesh side becomes too dry, it must be evenly dampened with a wet cloth before applying the tan liquor.

COMBINATION TANNAGE

A combination tannage is a combination of mineral and vegetable tanning. It has an advantage over the salt-acid or salt-alum processes in giving a soft and flexible skin, as well as a more lasting tannage. One of the most popular and successful formulas for a combination tannage is given by M. C. Lamb.[2] A pasty mixture of alum, salt, gambier, and flour, with or without glycerin or olive oil, is made as follows: Dissolve 1 pound of aluminium sulfate and 1 pound of salt together in a small quantity of water. Dissolve 3 ounces of gambier or Terra Japonica in a little boiling water. Mix the two solutions and make up to 2 gallons with water. As this solution is used, mix it with enough flour to make a moderately thin paste. If the skin has a hard texture and lacks natural grease, thoroughly mix a little olive oil or glycerin with the paste.

Soak, soften, and clean the skin as previously described and tack it out flat and smooth, flesh side up. Apply from two to three coatings of the paste, depending upon the thickness of the skin. Only thick skins require three coatings. Each coating should be about one-eighth inch thick and should be applied at intervals of a day. Between applications the skin should be kept covered with sacking or paper. Scrape off most of the old coating before putting on a new one. After the last coating has been applied, spread out the skin uncovered or hang it up to dry slowly.

When practically dry, wash off the flour paste, rinse for several minutes in water containing an ounce of borax to the gallon, then in water alone. Squeeze out most of the water. Put the skin over a beam and slick it out well on the flesh side with the back of a knife or edge of a wooden slicker (fig. 1), thus working out most of the water (fig. 7). Again tack the skin out smoothly, flesh side up, and apply a thin coating of any animal fat, fresh butter, being particu-

---

2 Leather Trades Review, August 20, 1913, p. 596.

TANNING

T ANNING is a process by which the hides and skins of various animals are changed by chemical action into leather. There are two distinct branches of this work which are known under the general term of tanning.

The first process to which the name tanning is often wrongly applied, is known as tawing, this includes the preparation of white leather by the action of such mineral substances as salt, alum, sulphuric acid, etc. Fur skins are always tanned by this process likewise the leathers which go to make kid gloves, moccasins and chamois. The second consists of the treatment, by immersion of hides in solutions containing tannic acid in various proportions. The leather produced by this process is used in the manufacture of shoes, harness and belts.

Tanning in all its branches entails a great deal of manual labor. There is no substance known that can be placed upon a hide that will turn it into leather without such labor, this is especially true of tawing or white leather dressing.

The tools which are required to successfully dress skins are few in number and not very expensive. A good skinning knife (Fig. 1), a fleshing knife (Fig. 4), and a currier's knife (Fig. 5). Two steels are necessary with this knife, the smaller one (Fig. 2) to keep the turned edge keen, and the large one (Fig. 3) to turn the edge of the blade.

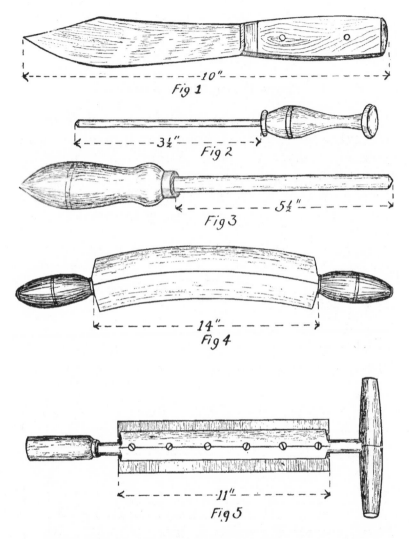

Fig 1

Fig 2

Fig 3

Fig 4

Fig 5

Although I am an advocate of good tools for good work, it is not always advisable to incur the expense of such unless the quantity of work demands it.

By careful attention to the working details in the illustrations anyone possessed of a little ability and ingenuity can make some very serviceable tools which will take the place of those which may be purchased ready made.

Some Home-Made Tools

To make a fleshing knife, procure a piece of an old scythe-blade 20 inches long and have the local blacksmith shape the ends so that they can be inserted in the handles (Fig. 6). If you have a forge of your own, so much the better. Do not heat any more of the ends than is necessary in this operation

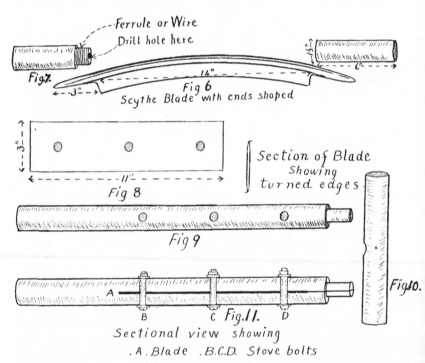

Fig.7. ----Ferrule or Wire Drill hole here

Fig 6 Scythe Blade with ends shaped

Fig 8

Section of Blade Showing turned edges

Fig 9

A Fig.11. B C D Fig.10.

Sectional view showing .A. Blade .B.C.D. Stove bolts

as it will interfere with the temper of the metal. Next procure two pieces of round hardwood 6 inches long and 1½ inches in diameter and bore a hole slightly smaller than the ends of the blade into them to the depth of 3 inches. These handles should first be bound with wire or a ferrule placed on the end, this prevents them splitting during the drilling or at any future time (Fig. 7).

To make a currier's knife, illustrated by Fig. 5, Plate 1, a piece of an old saw blade is secured 11 inches by 3 inches, this should be ground down until it is perfectly rectangular in form, as it is much better to have two cutting edges. This should be ground to a razor edge both sides being ground equally and well back. Previously have three holes punched along the center of this blade (Fig. 8, Plate 2), next procure a tough hardwood stick 1½ inches in diameter and 20 inches long, (Fig. 9) and another piece 9 inches long and the same diameter. Next with a brace and ¾ inch bit bore a hole through the centre of the 9 inch piece, (Fig. 10). Cut down the end of the 20 inch piece to ¾ inch diameter and 1½ inches from the end. With a saw make a cut straight down the center to within 6 inches of the uncut end. The small piece is now fixed to the end and fastened by means of a very fine screw or riveted with a piece of copper wire. Next drill three holes to correspond with those in the blade. Insert the blade and fasten with short stove bolts and washers, (Fig. 11). The edge of the blade must now be turned over. This is done with the large steel. Place the knife in a vise and by an even pressure, starting well back, gradually turn about one sixteenth of an inch of the blade at right angles to the rest (Fig. 8). When completed the knife should vary little in appearance and utility from the best currier's knife obtainable. A small finger steel can be made from a stout knitting needle. Make careful note of the shape of the point. The handle also is tapered toward the top so that it may be held between the fingers whilst using the knife. The purpose of this steel is to keep the turned edge keen by drawing it alternately back and forth. This is the reason for the shape of the point, that it may readily be drawn along the inner edge.

A turning steel can be made from an old rat tail file ground down quite smooth. Be sure of this, otherwise you will strip the edge when you start to turn. Should you be willing to spend the necessary time you can make a first class skinning knife of an old flat file ground down to the desired shape. A very good fleshing knife can be adapted from an ordinary carpenter's draw-knife, one with adjustable handles is the best. A common one will do providing the handles are straightened out (Fig. 12). This is used in the same manner as the other fleshing knife. I have found it very useful around such places as the eyes, nose and lips of hides where it is desirable to mount the head.

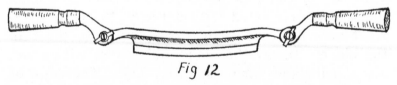

Fig 12

Adjustable draw-knife in shape for fleshing

Before we proceed with the work, it might be as well to explain that much of the manual labor connected with tanning is overcome in factories with the aid of machinery and various other devices. As many farmers now possess a motor for use in pumping, washing, churning, etc., and also as some of the contrivances used in fur dressing are not difficult nor expensive to construct it seems to be better to explain to the reader the methods used in a small plant which I once operated in connection with my other business of taxidermy. Some of the readers who are fortunate enough to have access to, or own a small motor and can obtain sufficient work in this line, will then be able to earn quite a little with this as a side line, while others will be able from the explanation, to devise various methods of doing the work by hand. For the benefit of all I will try and explain both methods as we proceed.

In commencing any tanning process the first step is to prepare the skin for fleshing. Fresh skins are better salted for a day or so and rolled up, flesh side in. This makes them flesh better. After this is done the salt is washed out in clear, soft water, the skin drained and the surplus water beamed out before applying the tan. Dried skins may be soaked in soft water until they are softened in every place, then drained, beamed out and fleshed. If there is any danger of the hair slipping or coming out through improper handling in the first place, they had better be laid on the floor, hair side down, and covered with wet sawdust on the flesh side. This will prevent the roots of the hair from being wet, and may save the skin from spoiling. In all cases soak hides where possible.

After purchasing or constructing the tools previously mentioned, the next thing necessary will be a beam, on which to flesh the skins. For all work except large hides it is best constructed as shown in Fig. 13. The size of this beam can be altered

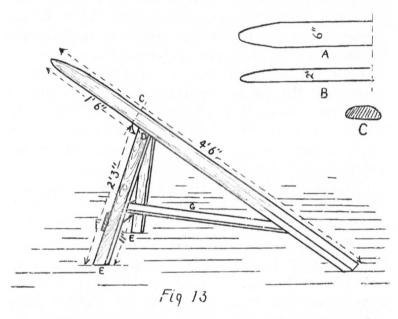

Fig 13

to suit the height of the person using it. The measurements given are all right for a person 5 feet 8 inches in height or thereabouts. To proceed, first secure a piece of hardwood plank, the closer the grain the better. This plank should be 2 inches by 6 inches by 4 feet 6 inches long, and the upper surface should be rounded almost its entire length. C shows how it should look in section at the place indicated by the dotted lines. It should also be pointed somewhat as shown by the top view

A and the side view B. The advantage of this will be seen when fleshing down the heads and feet of skins that have to be afterward mounted by taxidermic methods. Next fasten a short piece of wood 4 inches in length to the underside at the point marked D. This should be 1 foot 6 inches from the end. To this fasten the two legs E.E. 2 feet 3 inches long, and about 11 inches from the floor fasten a cross piece F. From this cross piece secure a stay as shown at G. All pieces must be firmly fixed with wood screws (not nails) and care should be taken that the ends of screws do not come near the upper surface of the beam, which must be perfectly smooth as the slightest unevenness will cause you to cut holes in the skin. The method of using the knife is shown on page 61. It must be held at a certain angle to work properly. This will be acquired by practice. It is pushed from the operator with a downward and slightly sideward motion. You will no doubt cut quite a number of holes before you get the hang of it. It would be advisable, therefore, to practice on some inexpensive hide to begin with. In place of the plank specified the beam may be made of a hardwood pole or a slab, the weight of the pole being in some respects an advantage in keeping the beam in place when working.

For larger hides a beam is made in exactly the same manner, the only difference being that it must be from 16 inches to 20 inches wide and not pointed at the end. It can be made from a large slab, a piece of wide plank, or from pieces of narrow hardwood flooring screwed to cleats as shown in Fig. 14.

The screws must be counter-sunk, the holes filled and the joints smoothed off.

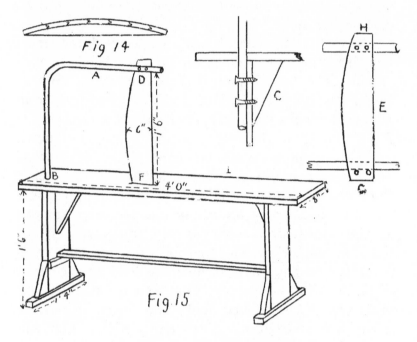

Fig 14

Fig 15

FLESHING SMALLER SKINS

The skins of muskrat, weasel, mink, marten and animals of a similar size are fleshed in a different manner. A bench should be constructed of 1 inch boards to the measurements given in Fig. 15. If desired the top can be of 2 inch plank and it may also be fitted with legs instead of the standards shown. When this is completed a piece of 1 inch iron pipe should be bent to the shape shown in A. Drill a hole in the bench at B and push the pipe through and fix as shown in the detail C. Two holes are drilled in the pipe for this purpose, two holes are also drilled at D and the end of the pipe split with a hack-saw. A knife should then be secured and drilled as shown in detail E. A piece of old saw blade will do for this. A cut should be made in the top of the bench at F by first drilling a hole and then making the cut with a pad-screw. The end of the blade G is now placed through this and retained by two bolts, and the other end H is fixed to the slit in the pipe also with two short bolts. The whole is adjusted so that the blade is taut. The blade must also be sharpened on the rounded edge previous to being fixed.

To flesh small skins in this manner the operator sits on the bench on the position marked I with one leg on each side and facing the back of the knife,

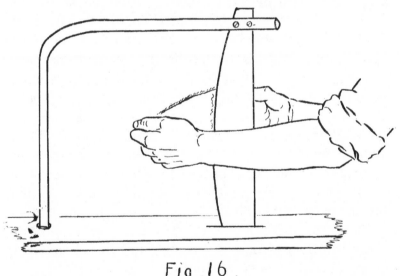

Fig 16.

passing the skin across the blade by drawing it with the right hand. The secret is to get the flesh and tissue that is to be removed, properly started, it then comes off readily. A skilled professional will remove the flesh on a rat in two strokes. If the novice tries to do this he will cut the skin in two. It is better to go easy at first. Fig. 16 shows the method of holding the skin. If you have only a few skins to do you can manage by placing the draw-knife upright in a vise, and drawing the skins over the edge in the same manner. In fleshing, while it is essential to get the skin as thin as possible, it must not be overdone, as if you cut too deep you will injure the roots of the hair and in the processes to follow it will either come right out or you will have as much hair on the inside as you do on the other. After being properly fleshed, the hides should be stretched on the floor, flesh side up, and swabbed over with a strong salt and sulphuric acid pickle, Taxidermy Formula No. 3. These ought to be left overnight and next morning swabbed again and rolled up, flesh side in. Repeat the next evening, and the following morning the skins should be hung up in a room with a temperature of about 100 degrees to dry. During this process do not allow them to dry thoroughly in any place. They should be taken out and beamed and broken or stretched every way until the whole skin is quite white and slightly moist and pliable all over. Then brush over with Neatsfoot oil, which penetrates quickly through the skin. In this condition they should be placed in a drum with hardwood sawdust and rotated for several hours.

A HOME-MADE REVOLVING DRUM

It is well to give here a description of this drum and a means of adapting it to the use of the amateur. The first drum we possessed was five feet in diameter and two feet six across.

Fig. 17 is a drawing of this drum, with the side taken out as it were, to show the interior fittings.

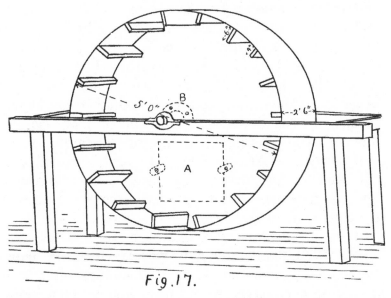

Fig. 17.

The circular sides were constructed of lumber well countered and with a door in one side as indicated by the dotted line at A. These sides were then fixed together with pieces of lumber alternately 6 inches and 4 inches wide as shown, the drum being then similar to a paddle wheel. A strip of strong galvanized iron was then fixed firmly around these paddles and sides with wood screws. The shafting did not extend through the drum but was fixed on the outside with plates as indicated by the dotted lines at B. The reason for having the inside of the drum free from shafting is so that the skins and sawdust, after being carried well to the top of the drum by the paddles, can fall with greater

47

force. This is essential for the proper breaking and cleaning of the skins.

The drum is raised about one foot from the floor as shown, and the shafting set in bearings. One end of this shafting was squared to fit a handle and the drum was then started slowly by hand. A pan containing burning charcoal was kept under the drum to supply the necessary heat when in operation. The whole arrangement was firmly fixed and braced and the galvanized iron especially was firmly screwed to the woodwork to prevent it from loosening with the constant pounding of the falling skins and sawdust. After being thoroughly cleaned and softened in the drum the skins were taken out and the sawdust beaten out with strong canes, and the fur combed and brushed into shape.

This entailed a lot of real hard work, so as soon as we were financially able we attached the drum to an electric motor with belt, pulleys, etc., and in addition constructed what is known as a cage, which is really another drum, constructed in exactly the same manner, with the exception that, in place of the galvanized iron it was encircled with heavy square 1 inch wire mesh. After being taken from the first drum, and the bulk of sawdust shaken out, the skins were placed in this cage which was then rotated. The pulleys being so arranged that the drum turned very slowly, allowing the skins to drop at each revolution, the sawdust dropping through the mesh to the floor beneath. This was continued until the furs were thoroughly cleaned. Needless to state there was no fire under this latter drum or cage. When taken out all that was necessary to complete the job was a light combing and beating.

Those who already possess a motor and can get sufficient of this work, would do well to construct such drums, and even if you have not a motor you can make a smaller drum to turn by hand: of course the taller the drum is the better, so much depending on the drop of the skins, etc. In some establishments they are ten feet in height. The one we constructed 5 feet high was some job for a husky man to turn for any length of time.

THE ARMSTRONG METHOD

Should you find it necessary to do all the work by hand, proceed as follows: First flesh the skin

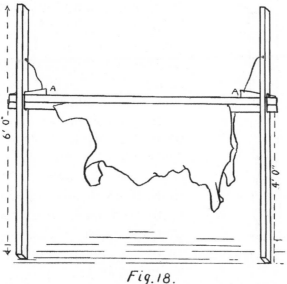

Fig. 18.

thoroughly as described, either by immersion of the hide in a tub or vat containing the liquor or by swabbing it on, or by applying in waste or powder form. Next hang the skin up to dry in the shade, and during the drying keep it thoroughly stretched and broken. The whole secret of success is to see that it does not become dry in any place until properly broken.

Large skins are worked over the beam with the knives, and small ones can be well broken by rubbing them over the edge of the knife as shown for fleshing in Fig. 16, or an old scythe blade may be placed in a vise and the skins worked over this. Another excellent device for breaking and stretching large skins is the Tanners Stretching Frame, Fig. 18. To make this, secure four pieces of 2x4

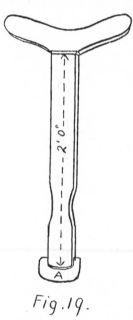

Fig. 19.

lumber six feet long and cut a mortise in two of them 4 feet from one end, and about 2 inches by 9 inches. This is to take the two cross pieces. Now cut two wedges AA and attach them with string to the uprights as shown. The hide is placed between the cross pieces and held in place with the wedges, the bottom cross piece is usually fixed in place with screws, but where there is not too much room it is better left loose, the frame can then be taken to pieces and put away in much smaller space when not in use.

The breaking is usually done with a moon knife which is a circular steel blade attached to a crutch. A more simply constructed stake knife can be made as shown in Fig. 19. It consists of a crutch to fit the arm and a piece of 1 inch board two feet long, and four inches wide. About six inches from the lower end it is shaped to fit the hand and a piece of steel is fitted into a saw cut in the end as shown A. The stick is mortised into the crutch to make the right arm, and the stick grasped at B. The edge of the skin being now grasped with the left hand, the skin is stretched by pressure with the steel A. The frame is leaned against a wall during this work.

SOME TANNING PREPARATIONS

Having described to the best of my ability the various devices used in dressing fur skins and white leather there remains but to give the few necessary formulas which I have successfully used.

The solution most extensively used in fur dressing is formula 3 (Taxidermy). Skins may be left in this solution anywhere from 2 days to a year or more, the longer they stay the better will be the tan. When this is used as a swab as directed previously, half the quantity of water should be used and the same amount of sulphuric acid and salt.

If the skins are to be finished entirely by hand they should be gone over on the flesh side when not quite dry with a little good coal oil instead of neatsfoot oil. If they are to be drummed, neatsfoot oil will be best. In all cases they must be thoroughly stretched, broken, and worked until quite dry.

In the Encyclopedia Britannica (ninth edition) is an article on Tanning. A system given there, which I will quote, I have successfully adapted to the dressing of skins by hand.

The quotation is as follows:—

"The tanning itself is accomplished in a drum or cylinder the same as a tanner's stuffing wheel, into which is introduced for one hundred average skins a mixture consisting of 20 pounds of alum, 9 pounds of salt, 40 pounds of flour, 250 eggs (or about 1 1/3 gallons of egg yolk, 7/8 pint of olive oil and 12 to 16 gallons of water. In this mixture at a temperature of not more than 100° F. the skins are worked for about 40 minutes, by which action the tanning is completed. After withdrawal from the drum the skins are allowed to drain, dried rapidly by artificial heat, damped, staked out by drawing them over a blunt steel tool, and then wetted and shaved down on the beam to the required thickness. Next they receive, if necessary, a second treatment with the tanning mixture."

I find that by reducing the quantities to the following and omitting the water excellent results are obtained.

> Alum ½ lb.
> Salt ¼ lb.
> Flour 1 lb.
> Eggs 6 lbs.
> Olive oil 3 teaspoons.

Mix to a thick paste with a little vinegar, and apply to flesh side of skin. Break, dry and stretch as usual.

An excellent leather may be obtained by mixing the above ingredients with about two quarts of water and immersing the skin. If necessary to make a larger quantity mix in proportion. Leave skin in two or three days, according to thickness, take out, hang up, dry, beam, etc.

One of the most simple methods is to mix together 1 pound of alum and 2 pounds of salt and pound it to a fine powder. After the hide has been thoroughly fleshed, rub this into the flesh side and roll the hide up flesh side in. Repeat this the next day and then hang the hide up to dry. Keep the hide thoroughly broken and stretched during the drying. One ounce of saltpeter added to the above ingredients will cause the tan to penetrate better. This is good for hides up to the size of a sheep or calf.

For larger hides it is better to make a pickle by boiling the above ingredients in 5 quarts of water, and then immersing the hides following the directions given in Making Robes. With these recipes you can successfully tan any kind of skins. The two main things to remember are — have the skin thoroughly fleshed, — don't allow the skin to dry out until thoroughly broken.

MAKING HORSE, COW AND SHEEP HIDE ROBES

If the hide is fresh it must first be salted on the flesh side and rolled up for a couple of days. Dry hides need to be soaked until quite soft.

The next process is fleshing. The salted hide is all right for this operation without further preparation. The dried hide after being soaked in water is drained thoroughly. They are then placed in the beam and every particle of flesh, fat, etc., is removed with the currier's knife. Unless this is attended to thoroughly you will not be able to make a good job of tanning the hide

It is next washed in clean water and soap and after being thoroughly drained and placed in the tan liquor (formula 3, Chapter on Taxidermy), it is stirred and turned every day until tanned. The time required will vary according to the hide, three or four days for a calf or sheep, and as much as two weeks for a horse or cow hide. When tanned it is taken out, drained, and washed again quickly in soap and water. The surplus water is then beamed out and the hide hung up to dry. As soon as a dry place appears it is pulled and stretched in every direction. No part of the hide is ever allowed to become dry, during the breaking. When thoroughly broken in every place and still damp to the touch, brush over the flesh side with kerosene or coal oil and break again. Repeat this operation as often as necessary, three or four times in the case of a large hide. When thoroughly tanned and pliable it is ready for the lining.

First proceed to repair all holes by the methods described in Rug Making, Chapter on Taxidermy, and then proceed to stretch the hide. This stretching is necessary in most cases on account of the fact that few hides will lay flat after being tanned, and are very difficult to line in this shape. It is advisable, therefore, to dampen the hide on the flesh side with warm water, and proceed to stretch it out on the floor or some suitable place (fur side up). Endeavor to work out every wrinkle and fold. It sometimes happens that there is still a fold in the flanks which no amount of stretching will take out. In this case this portion must be cut out and the edges of the cut sewn neatly together. The hide is held in place with small nails about three inches apart and driven in just enough to hold. When the hide is dry the nails are taken out and it is then trimmed to the desired shape. If the hide has stiffened it is rubbed soft again, by working over the beam or stretching frame lightly.

Robes are usually made with a double border of scalloped or pinked felt. Directions for making this will also be found in Rug Making (Chapter on Taxidermy). This is sewn to the edge of the hide, being gathered neatly at the corners to allow it to turn properly. If a good warm robe is desired it is better to interline with sheet cotton-batting. For a lining it is better to use a heavy blanket, plushette, or heavy blanket cloth. This is sewn to the felt edging close to the hide. If the robe is large it had better have several buttons of cloth sewn on the lining side and through the hide. This will hold the robe in better shape.

Tanning Leather

After soaking and fleshing the hide, as directed on page 73, it is ready for the lime. Following will be given ways for loosening fur, hair or wool. To keep hair or wool clean when taking it from hides take equal parts of hard wood ashes and slacked lime and make them into paste with soft water. Spread this on the flesh side of the skin, then fold flesh side together, roll it up and put in a tub, just covering it with water.

It should remain 10 days or until the hair comes out easily, then take to the fleshing beam and scrape off the hair. The currying knife shown in Fig. 14 is best for this purpose.

To loosen fur, hair or wool take eight quarts of slacked lime, add 10 gallons of soft water; then stir in nine quarts of hard wood ashes. Stir this liquid thoroughly and immerse the skins, which should be covered with the liquid. Let them soak three hours, then hang over the tub a few minutes to drain. Do this four times the first day, three times the second day and once a day until the hair starts on the thickest part, then rinse in clean water and scrape off the hair.

After the hair is taken off put the hide in clean water and let it soak half a day. Next let soak four hours in a liquid proportioned as follows: 24 quarts of soft water and eight quarts of sharp cider vinegar. Make only as much as is needed and throw away when done with it, as it is no good for future use. After soaking put the hides in soft water and scrape them on the fleshing beam three times in three days, removing all the fine hair. They are then ready for the tan liquor.

Several ways of tanning are given, but hides should be treated as above directed until ready for the tan.

THE COMPLETE PROCESS

Take 32 quarts of Mayweed and bark liquor,[1] 1 ounce of pulverized alum, 1 ounce of pulverized salt, ¼ ounce of saltpeter, 3 pounds of Terra Japonica. Dissolve the Japonica in water before putting it in. Stir well until all is dissolved, then put in the hides and let them soak one day, occasionally pulling them out and working with the hands. During the first

---

[1] **How to Get Bark Liquor for Tanning.**—Break the barks, shrubs, herbs and plants into small pieces and put them into a large kettle or boiler, cover with water and let steep until the strength comes out of the barks. It matters not about the amount of each kind as long as you have some of each, but have enough of all together to make good strong liquor. When using bark liquor for tanning if it gets weak put it back into the boiler with the barks and herbs and let steep again. When Japonica liquor gets weak put in more Japonica. The way to make Japonica liquor is to break it up fine and put it into the amount of water you need, then stir until dissolved

day make a liquid by steeping Tansy, Smartweed, Spearmint, Sweet-fern and barks, make 40 gallons of this and then put into it dissolved 1 ounce of alum and 1 ounce of salt. The second day put the hides into this liquid and haul them out two or three times. Next day put the hides back into the Japonica liquor. Change them this way from one tub to the other every day until tanned, letting them hang up each time long enough to drain. If smaller quantities are required reduce all ingredients in proportion.

If Mayweed is not obtainable you can use Smartweed, Tansy, Sweet-fern and Spearmint in its place, either separately or all together; and if you can not get any of the above named herbs and plants for the second, or 40 gallons liquid, you may use two pounds of Terra Japonica and one pound of extract of Hemlock. If you use the Japonica and Hemlock make 40 gallons of it and then put in the alum and salt same as with the herbs and plants.

The above liquor should be strengthened occasionally by adding Japonica to the Japonica liquor and returning the bark liquor into leach for more strength. If the liquors are weak the leather will be poor. Hides in weak liquor grow slippery while those in strong liquor feel rough to the hands on the grain side.

When these hides are tanned hang them up to drain; then lay on the table and oil the grain side with any suitable oil, as Neat's-foot, tanner's oil, and hang in the shade to dry. Dip them in water so as to make them just damp enough for skiving, after which scour well. Skiving is the term used by professionals to describe a process which resembles the first fleshing and which reduces all unevenness in the thickness of the leather.

SCOURING

To scour the hides put them in a tub of water then lay on table, flesh side up; take a stiff brush and apply it faithfully to the leather, then sleek the water and filth off with an iron sleek. Dip in water again and lay on the table, grain side up, (grain side means, side hair was on) and apply brush as before; then apply stone sleek faithfully to work down every wrinkle. With a cup throw water over the leather and finish scouring by applying the brush and iron sleek, sleeking the water out as dry as possible. The next thing to do is to stuff the leather with stuffing proportioned as follows: Make four pounds of beef tallow hot and pour it into six quarts of tanner's oil, stir occasionally; when nearly cold stir into it two gills best kerosene oil. Just before stuffing the leather, oil the grain side, put oiled side on the table and then with an iron sleek, sleek down the leather every way smoothly. Then with a soft brush apply the stuffing evenly over the flesh side, leaving it one-third as thick as the leather. Take a bunch of horse hair, mane or tail, and rub off every particle of stuffing from the grain of the leather. Next take it on the whitening beam and with the whitening knife take a shaving from every part of the flesh side, making it completely smooth. This can be done with good sharp sleek on table. Then sleek off the grain with stone sleek. Next lay the leather on the table, flesh side down, and commence at one corner of the leather with grain board in right hand, and grain or bowl the leather diagonally across two ways. The tool used for this purpose is a flat piece of board about 5 inches by 10 inches with a strap across the back in which to place the hand, after the manner of a circular curry comb. Its working surface is corrugated across the short way. The leather is now ready for the Blacking.

Put the leather on the table, and with a stiff brush apply faithfully to the flesh side the blacking, proportioned as follows: two quarts of tanner's oil, one ounce of lamp black, stir well, then stir into this half pint Japonica liquor. After this blacking has dried, rub the blacked side over with a clean woolen cloth to remove all loose particles; and with a soft brush apply evenly a paste made as follows: Two quarts boiling rain water, a few shavings of hard soap and two-thirds pint of thickening made of fine flour and soft water well stirred in; let it boil a few minutes, then let it cool; stir into this paste ¼ as much melted Gum Tragacanth. When this paste is dried into the leather, take it on the table and sleek the black side over with a sharp glass sleek. Then make another paste same as first only stir in twice as much gum as the first, put it on with a fine sponge. When dry, sleek to finish with glass sleek. This completes the finish on the flesh side.

Grain Blacking

Put into an iron vessel a quantity of old iron; then put 4 ounces of extract logwood into a gallon of sharp cider vinegar, dissolve over a slow fire; when dissolved pour it into the old iron and cover tight; the longer it stands the better it is. When blacking is wanted, set a deep stone jar in an open room and put in 4 ounces copperas, and 2 ounces logwood; then pour in aquafortis enough to dissolve the copperas and logwood; immediately cover tight, and when dissolved put it into 2 quarts of the vinegar from the old iron. Next heat and keep hot a quantity of zeig; apply the hot zeig with a stiff brush to the grain of the leather and when moistened enough, apply the blacking with a brush. When nearly dry set the blacking down smoothly with a stone sleek; then with an iron sleek remove all the stuffing from the flesh side, and with old woolen cloths clean the blackened side of smut; stuff with hot tallow the blacked side and hang up to dry. When dry sleek the tallow from the blacked side and to finish, polish by applying old woolen rags with energy. If the work has been done as directed, no better leather was ever made than you have just completed.

A Shorter Process

Take 12 ounces of salt; 2 ounces saltpetre; 3 pounds Terra Japonica. Dissolve the above articles in water, and put it into 8 quarts of whey; stir well, then pour in 4 ounces of Sulphuric Acid. Stir thoroughly, in this liquid immerse the skins. Handle well, and strengthen the liquor when necessary. Always use the same proportions when making more or less liquid. Thin skins will tan in a few days; heavier skins up to fifteen days. When tanned finish as above directed.

A Thirty to Sixty Day Process

The amount given is for a 12-pound calf skin: Put in a copper kettle (if you haven't copper, tin will do) with 20 quarts water, 1 pound alum, 2 pounds salt, 3 pounds Terra Japonica, and dissolve without boiling. Put the skin in a tub and cover it with water, then put in one pint of the tan liquor and stir well. Add one pint of the liquor every night and morning for three days, stirring well every time; then put in all the liquor that remains. Handle the skin two or three times daily while tanning. You can continue to use the tanning liquid by adding half the quantity each time for any amount. Always keep same proportions.

If you wish to make dark leather put in one pound of Sicily Sumac. Horsehides for harness will require about 30 days, kip skins 20 days and calf skins from six to ten days at most. To make good mitten leather, leave out the Sicily Sumac and when tanned, scour or wash in water, then soak 40 minutes in real warm boiled oil hang up to dry and work while drying by pulling and rubbing with the hands. When dry it is ready for use.

Tanning Raw Hide in Twenty Minutes

Take 1½ pints Sulphuric Acid and pour it slowly into 1½ pints soft water (this amount for a common sized cow hide). Put the hide, flesh side up, on the table and thoroughly wet the flesh side with the acid and water by means of a cloth or sponge tied to a stick. Fold flesh sides together and let it stand only 20 minutes, having ready a solution of soda and water, one pound of soda to 16 quarts of water, and let the skin soak in this 2 hours; then wash in clean water and apply a little dry salt, letting it lie in the salt 12 hours. Take to beam and remove all the flesh, and soak a few minutes in water, then sponge onto the flesh side, Neatsfoot oil, and hang up to dry; work well while drying. When dry it is ready for use.

Great care must be taken when pouring Sulphuric Acid into water or when allowing it to come into contact with certain soda compounds. When mixing sulphuric and water, have a container for the water deeper than what is needed to hold it actually. Then tip slightly and pour acid gently down the lower side of the container, stirring slowly meanwhile. Never pour water into acid nor acid directly on water. Acid and soda solutions should never be mixed but no violent reaction occurs if the above instructions are followed and the hide is first treated with one and then immersed in the other.

Deer Skins for Gloves

For each skin take 12 quarts of water and put into it one quart of lime; let the skin soak in this 3 or 4 days, then rinse in clean water and scrape off the hair. After scraping soak in cold water two days, and scour or pound in good soap suds half an hour; then take white vitrol, alum and salt; one tablespoon of each to a skin, dissolve them in enough water to cover and let the skin soak in this 24 hours, then wring out as dry as possible. When dry spread on with a brush, ½ pint tanner's oil and hang in the sun for 2 days. Next scour out the oil with soap suds and hang out again until perfectly dry;

then pull and rub the skin until soft. If a reasonable time does not make them soft, scour out again in suds until complete. The buff color is given by yellow ochre spread evenly over the skin and rubbed well with a brush.

DEER SKINS FOR GRAINING

Make the skin perfectly soft by soaking, then prepare a weak lime as follows: 8 gallons soft water and 4 quarts slacked lime; stir thoroughly and immerse the skin. Handle well the first day; the second day handle twice; the third day take out and rinse in clean water. After rinsing take to beam and scrape off a narrow strip of the hide with the hair at every motion of the grain knife. After working all the grain off, soak them in equal parts of Citric Acid and soft water for one hour. Next throw the skin into soft water and work twice on beam, scraping the flesh side; the skin is then ready for the tan liquor as follows: Take the brains from two deer or hog's heads and put them into 8 quarts of tepid soft water, stir until dissolved (make enough of this liquid to cover the skin and keep the same proportions); immerse the skin, and let it soak for one hour, then hang in the shade to dry; when dry immerse again and let it soak half a day; then wring all the liquid out of them. Next run them over the stake knife every way to stretch, and hang up to dry. While drying pull every way to soften. Repeat the operation until tanned and soft, which will be about four times soaking. After the fourth or last wringing, while damp, sponge on a coat of kerosene oil. When dry hang in a smoke house and smoke until the skin is a cream color. (For smoke, burn maple or birch punk or decayed wood.) To finish rub with pumice stone.

GLOVE LEATHER

Calf, dog, lamb, or cat skins for this purpose may be limed and haired same as given on page 83 or as follows:

Dissolve 1 pound of potash in 10 gallons of soft water, add to this 8 quarts slacked lime and 8 quarts hard wood ashes, stir well and immerse the skins. Handle constantly, for the wool will start within two hours; hair will start in from three to nine hours. After the wool or hair is taken off and the flesh all scraped off, handle in equal parts of sharp cider vinegar and water for two hours. Next soak in soft water and scrape each skin twice on the beam, when they are ready for the tan liquid as follows:

32 quarts soft water; 4 pounds Terra Japonica; 4 pounds Glauber salts; 4 pounds alum; 1 pound salt. Stir until all are dissolved. Handle well. The lamb skins will tan in one hour.

REMOVING WOOL

Soak until very soft. Dissolve 2 ounces of potash in one gallon of soft water, and with this make a paste of equal parts of lime and hard wood ashes. Spread on the flesh side, roll flesh sides together and lay skin in damp place. Wool will start in two hours.

TANNING

Tanning or leathering animal skins and hides requires manual labor more than a knowledge of many formulas and "secret" methods. There are no known methods of tanning today by which some "secret" solution can be applied to the raw skins to turn them out beautifully tanned and ready for use. A well-tanned skin is soft and pliable over its entire surface and has plenty of "life," or stretch to it. Successful tanning requires years of working experience in the handling of skins to get the "feel" of the work; to know just what to do and when to do it. The important process of beaming or working the skin to break up tiny fibers is where the elements of manual labor and skill enter into the process.

Tools

The tools required are not many. They can be made or, which is preferable, bought from a taxidermy supply company. Not expensive to buy, the proper tools facilitate the work. The necessary tools are shown in Figure 92. They are, left to right, two skinning knives, steel (for sharpening knives), small shaving beam, currier's knife, and scraping knife.

The currier's knife can be made from part of an old saw blade. Grind the blade until it is rectangular in shape with wide bevels and drill three holes along the center line (Figure 93, A). Next, secure a 20-inch length of hardwood 1½ inches in diameter, and another piece 6 inches in length, of the same diameter. Bore a ¾-inch hole part way through the center of the shorter piece and fit into it one end of the longer piece. Slit the latter with a handsaw from that end straight through the center to a point 6 inches from the opposite end. Slip the blade into the

FIGURE 92

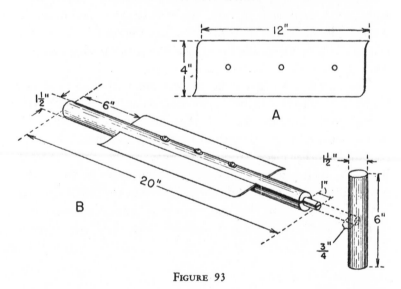

FIGURE 93

slot and bore holes in the wood to correspond with those in the blade (Figure 93, B). Drive the handle on and pin or rivet it in place. Finally, sharpen both cutting edges of the blade with a large knife steel in the same way that the edge of a floor or cabinet scraper is turned. This currier's knife is used for fleshing all large skins.

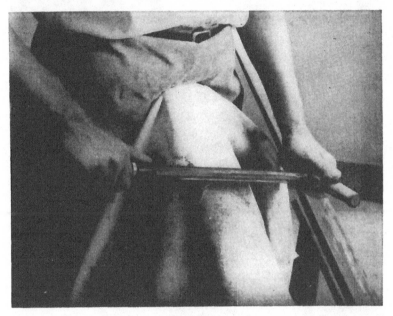

FIGURE 94

Figure 94 illustrates the proper way to hold the knife when shaving heavy skins. One must be careful to hold it at the correct angle and apply the proper pressure, lest a cut be made in the skin. This skill is learned by experience. The knife will become dull with use and must be honed to keep the cutting edge at the uniform sharpness necessary to thin the skin evenly. Figure 95 illustrates the proper technique of honing the knife to give the cutting edge an all-over sharpness.

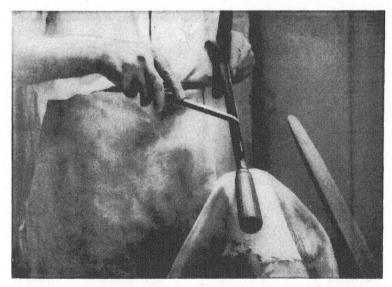

FIGURE 95

FIGURE 96

Figure 96 shows an upright fleshing knife, for work on smaller skins, being used to shave a skin. This knife can either be purchased from a taxidermy supply company or made at home

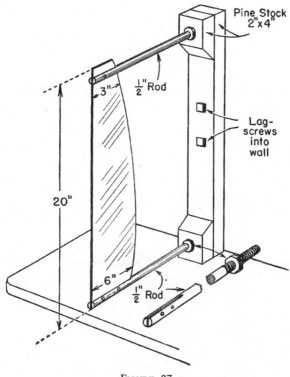

Pine Stock
2"x4"

3" ½"Rod

Lag-
screws
into
wall

20"

6"

½" Rod

FIGURE 97

from an old saw blade by filing off the teeth and grinding and honing the edge. It should be supported on a bench and bolted to the wall. In making this upright knife, follow the measurements specified in Figure 97, making sure to anchor the knife to a solid support so that it is held securely.

Although you have been instructed on how to make the different knives used in thinning down skins, if you plan to do a lot of this kind of work it is much better to purchase these knives. They will give better results.

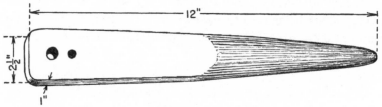

FIGURE 98

Fleshing Beams

Before the tanning can be started, several fleshing beams must be available to support the skin while the flesh side is shaved. The small beam, shown in Figure 98, can be whittled from a piece of hardwood about 12 inches in length, 2½ inches in width and 1 inch in thickness. Shape the end to a blunt point and round over the top sides so that the skins will slide easily while being shaved. Figure 99 shows a small skin being worked over the small fleshing beam.

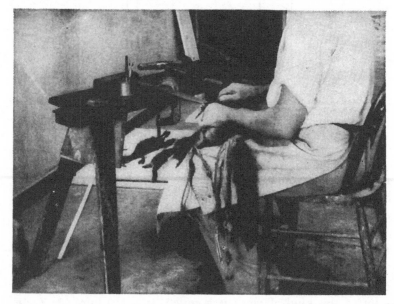

FIGURE 99

70

The heavier beam, shown in Figure 100, is constructed from a plank of hardwood 5 feet in length, 10 inches in width, and 1½ inches in thickness. The upper edges are rounded off over the full length. The height of this beam can be varied to suit the individual worker. The way in which heavier skins are worked over this beam is shown in Figure 101.

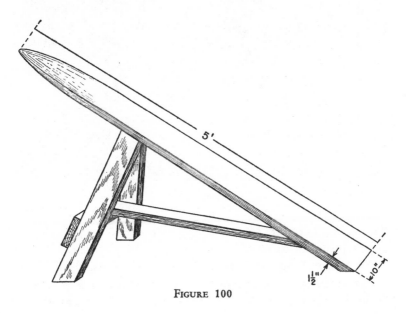

FIGURE 100

Preparing the Skins

All skins must be shaved and degreased before the tanning solutions can take effect. Before the skins are shaved or fleshed, however, certain preliminary steps must be followed. As soon as the skin is removed from the animal's body, the nostrils, lips, and area around the eyes are split open, and the ears turned inside out by splitting them open between the cartilage and skin (Figure 77). This step is very important since the solutions will not act on any part of the skin if the flesh is left on. The skin is now salted with common salt until the entire flesh side of

FIGURE 101

the skin is thoroughly covered. It is then rolled up, flesh side in, and left undisturbed for several days.

Skins which have been received in a dry, hard condition can be soaked in water containing a small amount of carbolic acid, Formula #104, until pliable. This will also keep them free of bacteria which cause the hair to slip. Should a skin become too soft and limp in this solution, add a little salt.

After the skin has been salted and laid away, it will be found to have dried out and become wrinkled. To restore it to the proper condition for shaving, it must be soaked overnight in a fairly strong solution of salt water containing a small amount of carbolic acid, and allowed to drain.

It is very important that all skins be shaved or fleshed until they are as thin as possible. No skin can be tanned so that it will stretch properly unless it is shaved thoroughly before the application of the tanning solutions. Experience is the important requirement at this stage of the tanning operation.

Degreasing

When all muscle and tissue have been shaved off and the skins are of the desired thickness any remaining fat must be degreased. To do this, soak smaller skins in naphtha solution thoroughly. Large skins are stretched out on the floor, naphtha sprinkled on both flesh and hair sides, and coarse hardwood sawdust rubbed in and worked well into the hair to absorb the naphtha and grease. Now shake or beat out all sawdust and wash the skin thoroughly in several rinses of clear water to remove any traces of salt remaining in the skins. Next, drain, but do not dry, the skin, and proceed with the tanning process.

Tanning

After the skins are thoroughly shaved or fleshed, degreased, and washed clean of all salt, they are stretched out on the floor, flesh side up, and wet down with a coating of the pickling solution, Formula #111. Next, sprinkle a small amount of sawdust over the flesh and repeat the application of the pickle, making certain that all parts of the skin are well covered. The sawdust will absorb some of the solution and keep it from running off the skin. Leave the skins stretched out on the floor overnight to allow the solution to penetrate through the flesh side, but do not let the skin dry out. Finally, the flesh side is covered with a coat of sulphonated neat's-foot-oil solution, Formula #112.

Now hang the skin up until it is thoroughly dry. Then dampen it with a solution of carbolic-acid-water. Roll it up, flesh side in, and lay it away overnight. The next day, the skin will be ready to be worked with the hands over the large beam. This work consists of stretching the skin in every way until it is soft and pliable. Again, hard work is called for. The skins must be worked until they have plenty of "life" and stretch.

Cleaning the Fur

After the skin has been thoroughly worked, lay it hair side up on the floor and sprinkle on a small amount of naphtha. Be careful that the naphtha does not get on the flesh side, for it will remove the oil. Now rub in sawdust to dry and cleanse the hair. After the sawdust has been worked into the hair or fur and has absorbed the naphtha, beat it out with a small, flexible stick. This will also serve to "fluff" up the hair. (Heavier hides must be dampened once again after this with the carbolic-acid-water solution, rolled up, and put away overnight. The next day these hides are pliable and in proper condition for a final shaving over the fleshing beam.) Use extreme care at this stage against putting any cuts in the skin. Lay the skin on the floor once more and sponge on a mild solution of warm, soapy water. Then roll it up, flesh side in, and lay it away overnight. The next day it may be necessary to give the skin another light coat of the sulphonated oil. The tanning process is now complete. The skin should be soft and pliable enough for mounting or for being made into a rug.

Tanning with Alum

Tanning with alum is an easier method to leather skins. Although an old method, it is still used today by many professional tanners.

Small skins that have been dried without preservatives and those that have been salted must be relaxed by covering the flesh side with sawdust dampened with carbolic-acid-water solution. (Large or thick skins must be immersed in the solution to accomplish this.) After they are pliable, shave, degrease, and clean them as previously described. Then immerse in the alum solution, Formula #113.

After leaving the skins in this solution for about a week, remove them and allow them to drain. After draining, apply a coat of the sulphonated-oil-water solution and allow the skin to dry thoroughly. Then relax the skins once more with carbolic-acid-water solution and work them over the beam to make them pliable. If a particularly fine job of tanning is desired, the skins can again be shaved, oiled, and allowed to dry. When dry, dampen once more and, again, gradually work them over the beam until pliable. When they are cleaned with sawdust, the job is finished. If the skins have been well handled throughout the tanning process they will be, at this time, white all over the flesh side and very supple.

Tanning Without the Hair

To tan a skin and, at the same time, remove the hair or fur, the skin must be first soaked and fleshed and then placed in the solution, Formula #114. This will remove all the hair and leave the skin well cleaned on both sides. (Be sure that the skin is free of all dirt, salt, and fat, before placing it in this solution.) Be careful to soak the skin until the hair is loose and can be slipped or scraped off easily. The skin can be laid over the fleshing beam and the hair pushed off with the currier's knife. If the hair does not come off easily, put the skin back into the solution once more. Remove, drain, and wash it out in warm water to remove the lime. Then neutralize any remaining lime by soaking the skin overnight in the solution, Formula #115. Work the skin occasionally with the hands in the solution. Remove the skin and wash it thoroughly in several changes of clear water. Proceed with the tanning of the skin as described, but add 15 grams of chrome alum (dissolved) to the tanning liquid.

Tanning Snake Skins

The tanning of snake skins can be the most disappointing of all tanning jobs. This is due to several difficulties which vary with the type of skin being worked. Many formulas have been tried and new ones are being worked out all the time, but few are entirely successful. The following method, however, can be used for a number of skins.

If the skin is not fresh from the specimen, soak it in water until soft. The skin then is fleshed and put in a solution of lime and water, Formula #116. Allow the skin to soak for two or three days, or until the scales are loose, but not any longer. Now scrape away all scales with a stiff brush. (Snake skins cannot be successfully tanned with the scales remaining on the skin.) Before proceeding any further, it is most important to remove all lime from the skin. Do this by soaking it in the solution, Formula #115. Work the skin through this solution several times. Now make a weak solution of alum and salt, Formula #117. Place the skin in this solution and allow it to remain for three to four days. Dissolve 5 grams of sodium carbonate in a glass of warm water and add this to the solution, drop by drop, taking about twenty minutes to add it all. Keep the skin in this solution for six days, stirring once or twice each day.

Now remove the skin from the liquid, drain it, and soak it overnight in a weak solution of sulphonated oil (1 part oil to 3 parts water). Squeeze the liquid out of the skin, stretch it, and tack it on a board so that it can dry thoroughly. When dry, take it off the board and gently work it over the fleshing beam until it is soft and pliable. When the skin is dry and pliable, it must be gone over with a warm iron in the same way as a suit is pressed. Finally, apply a thin coat of liquid celluloid to the pattern side of the skin to give to it a new and glossy look.

Conclusion

Successful results in taxidermy can only be achieved by many hours of hard work and many years of practical experience. In a book of this kind, all that can be done is to give the methods and techniques to follow in the mounting of birds, mammals, and fish. Even while these techniques are being mastered, many hours should be spent in the study of living birds and animals, either in the wild state, or in zoos.

It is only by a combination of knowing what to do and the results wanted that one can become an experienced taxidermist. The outcome of a well-mounted bird or animal depends entirely on, first, your knowledge of the animal as it was in life, and, second, your experience in mounting that animal to look alive.

How to Tan Skins

Every collector should have a knowledge of at least one good method of tanning furs and skins in such a way that the hair and fur will not slip, and so that the skin itself will be nice, **soft and pliable.** We have given a great deal of time and investigation to the subject of amateur tanning and have come to the following conclusions:

Small and medium hides can be tanned with complete satisfaction by several processes, and this work can be done in the home without sending the skins away to a regular tannery. Very **large** and **heavy hides,** such as buffalo, elk, cow, horse, etc., are **very difficult to tan** without the special equipment and machinery found in a regular tannery. It does not justify one to buy this machinery, unless he is actually going into the tanning business. While heavy hides can be tanned fairly satisfactory by hand methods, etc., we wish the student to understand that he must not expect to make as good a job as the fully equipped tannery turns out. These skins are so heavy and difficult to handle and break up that it is almost impossible for one to do the work right by hand. We, however, give you instructions on how to get fair results even with heavy hides.

Small and Medium-Sized Hides
FIRST METHOD

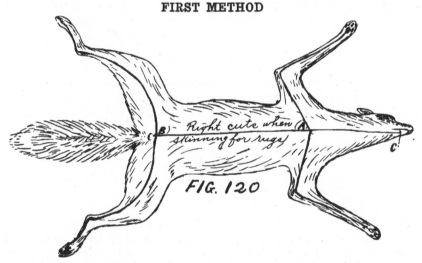

FIG. 120

We present a number of different formulas that have been proven and found satisfactory for all skins up to the size of a deer, wolf, small bear, coyote, and all smaller animals. The **first method,** which we explain in detail, is without doubt the **most satisfactory, and we recommend it to the use of our students.** We give the other methods simply because they have some good points, but under ordinary conditions the best results will be secured from the **first method.**

Choice skins and furs are usually secured while the collector is away from home on his outing, and he has neither the time nor opportunity to tan the skins while fresh. They must then be dried and tanned at some future time.

When small skins are secured, such as the squirrel, coon, fox, etc.,
remain for a few hours.
they should be cleansed from all clinging flesh and fat and tacked to a
flat surface after being thoroughly stretched, and covered with an application of common salt. They will soon dry, but will be hard and stiff.
In this condition they can be packed together and shipped with no fear of
injury. Larger skins should be tacked down flesh side up and literally
loaded with salt. They must be kept in the shade, yet in a dry place, so
that they will become properly cured. Apply the salt frequently if they
do not dry properly after the first application.

Figure 120 indicates clearly the proper cuts to make when skinning
animals for rugs and robes. First cut from "A" to "C" and then make
the leg cuts from the points "A" and "B" entirely to the feet.

Relaxing Dried Skins for Tanning

When you desire to tan a dry, hard skin, either large or small, it
must first be **carefully prepared.** In order to tan properly it is necessary
to **thoroughly relax the skin and make it soft** before you apply the tanning liquor. If the skin is hard and dry and has considerable flesh on it,
you should place it over a beam and go over the interior with a currier's knife, breaking up the hardest and roughest parts before you start
to soak it up, and then put the skin in a vat of water and allow it to

Fig. 121

Examine it frequently and you will probably find that it is soaking
up in some spots faster than in others. Remove it from the water and
shave down the hard spots and then put it back in the water and allow
it to soak again. Repeat the shaving operation on the hard places, thus
helping the skin to soak up as quickly as possible. **Do not leave the hide
in the water too long, or the hair is apt to slip,** therefore soften it as soon
as you can. When you take it out of the water break up the stiffness of
the skin with a fleshing knife and currier's knife while the skin is over
a beam. If one part of the skin seems to get softer than the others, then
you should simply soak the stiff end in water, leaving the soft outside, for
as stated above, you can very easily spoil the skin by leaving it in water
until the hair slips, and when it does slip, there is no known method of
setting it.

Some skins are so flinty that it is difficult to relax them by soaking
in water. In such cases put sulphuric acid in the water in the proportion

of 2 ounces of acid to 5 gallons of water. Leave the skin in until the flinty places become soft and spongy.

Nothing except **good hard work** and close attention will enable you to properly soak up a dried skin and get it in suitable condition for tanning. Whichever method you use in tanning, you should keep the following fact in mind: **A skin cannot be successfully tanned until it has been shaved down thin.** This is **imperative.** Not only the clinging fat and flesh must be removed, but you must actually **shave** the whole interior of the hide so that the tanning liquor can soak into the skin freely in all places.

More skins are spoiled by trying to tan them **before they are ready** than by all other means. In fact, the hardest work of all in tanning skins is to get them in **good condition.** Keep this in mind at all times, and **REMEMBER** that a hard, flinty skin can **never** be tanned until it has been soaked up and shaved down and made soft on every square inch of the surface.

On the other hand, care must be used with some skins, especially bear, raccoon and badger, not to shave them so thin that you will cut off the roots of the hair, causing the hair to come out. There is not so much danger of this in shaving a prime hide, as the roots of the hair are not so deep as in an unprime or "blue" hide. **Fox skins are so thin that no shaving is required.**

Preparing the Tanning Liquor

After you have the skin in first-class condition, you can prepare the solution which does the actual tanning. This tanning liquor is made from **salt, sulphuric acid and water.**

Prepare as Follows:

Secure the required quantity of rain water **or** soft water to make the desired amount of tanning liquor. For each gallon of water you should use about **2 pounds** of common salt. If you wish 5 gallons of liquor you should of course use 9 to 10 pounds of **salt.** Stir the salt into the water and continue to stir until it **is fully dissolved.** Perhaps all of the salt will not dissolve, but stir the solution until the water has taken up all the salt that it will and becomes fully saturated.

Now pour into this brine **about 3 ounces of common commercial** sulphuric acid, such as you can procure at any drug store, for every five gallons of brine.

It is not necessary to use chemically pure acid; simply tell your druggist that you want common commercial acid and he will know just what you need. Stir the acid well into the brine and you will now have the tanning liquor complete. It is a good plan to keep this liquor in air-tight jars or large bottles. You are now ready to tan the hide, which has already been carefully prepared.

The Actual Tanning

Stretch the skin out and tack it on the floor on a large board. It is not necessary to stretch the skin very tightly at this time, but it should be so spread out that every part of the interior is exposed.

Now pour a small quantity of the tanning liquor in the center of the hide and spread it out by the use of a stick on which you have tied a wad of waste, or soft cloth. With this swab spread the **tanning liquor** over **all parts of the interior of the skin.**

If necessary pour on a little more from time to time, until you are sure that each and every part of the inside of the skin has been covered. Get it on entirely to the edges, but do not get it on the hair.

It is a good plan to scatter a little sawdust on the skin so that the tanning liquor will not settle in a few places only, or run off the edges of the hide.

Small hides will require only one application of the tanning liquor, but very heavy ones should have another application after half an hour.

Leave the skin stretched out for half an hour and then **ROLL IT UP WITH THE FLESH SIDES TOGETHER.** Lay it away for about 12 hours, and then examine it. Stretch it with the hands and if it shows **WHITE** all over, the tanning is done. If it appears raw in spots, then roll it up again and leave it a few hours longer. Experience will soon tell you when it is done.

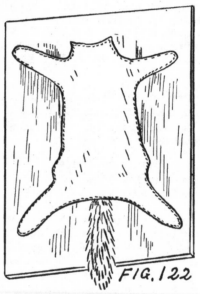

FIG. 122

Now hang the hide up and allow it to become dry. After it is dry or almost so, spread it out and wet the leather side well with **soap suds,** and roll it up carefully and allow it to remain until it is thoroughly soft again. This will require 12 hours or more. After this put the hide, while still wet, on the beam and break it up with the fleshing knife, and if necessary use the currier's knife to soften any hard or stiff places.

Oiling the Hides

If you are tanning skins with very heavy leather, such as badger, raccoon, calfskin, etc., instead of applying soap suds as just described, use a mixture of neatsfoot oil and soap suds and apply this while the skin is still wet, as follows: Dissolve 2 pounds of soap in 1 gallon of water. Heat till it boils. Then pour in $\frac{1}{2}$ gallon of neatsfoot oil, which will make an emulsion. Apply this mixture to the leather side with a

80

brush until it is well covered. If a smaller quantity is desired, use a less amount of each ingredient in the same proportion. Nail the skin up and this mixture will soak into the leather, and while it is still somewhat moist, break up any hard places with a fleshing knife.

A spoonful of sal soda in the above mixture will assist in conditioning the hide by somewhat neutralizing the acid used in the tan.

The skin is now ready for the last process of the tanning, which further breaks up the stiffness, and also cleanses the hair or fur.

Tubbing the Hides

We now wish to describe briefly what professional tanners term "tubbing." This is a treatment that softens the skins after tanning, and if the student can arrange to "tub" the skins, the results will be exceedingly gratifying. In order to do this, you will need no equipment except a barrel or tub, and about a bushel of hardwood sawdust. The skins are placed in the barrel while moist and covered liberally with the sawdust, and then simply manipulated by tramping with the bare feet. It is best to have several small skins treated at the same time. Have plenty of sawdust and continue to tramp the skins, turning them in all positions, with first one side up, then the other, for half an hour to an hour, and by that time all hardness, stiffness, etc., will have completely disappeared. This seems a crude way to perform the work, yet in all small tanneries will be found professional "tubbers."

After "tubbing" you should then work the skin over a beam again until it becomes perfectly soft and pliable in all parts.

After you have the hides "tubbed" you may discover that some parts are still stiff and hard, and if so, you should work them over a beam and "tub" them again. It is a good plan to "tub" the hides a second time in order to make them soft and clean. Before the second "tubbing," use coarse sandpaper on the skin. It is by liberal use of sandpaper that professional tanners secure the smooth appearance of the leather.

When the skin is taken from the tub for the last time you can then hang it up and beat it for a considerable time in order to remove all the sawdust from the hair. It is then of course necessary to comb and brush the hair until it is perfectly soft and fluffy. A good currier's comb is absolutely necessary for this class of work.

You should now have a nicely finished skin that is well tanned. If you are at all successful with your first efforts, you should congratulate yourself. A few efforts, however, will enable you to get good results, and if you follow these instructions closely, there is no reason why you should not tan skins with complete satisfaction for rugs and robes.

After the skin is finished, you may dampen it slightly with soap suds, and wrap it again for an hour or two, after which you can stretch it on the floor lightly and tack the edges, as shown on figure 122. This will straighten it out so it will lie smoothly when made into a rug or robe.

Caution—The tanning liquor is a poison and should be treated accordingly. Do not get the acid on the hands or clothes; simply use ordinary caution with the tanning liquor and there is no danger whatever.

Preserving the Ears

Special attention should be given to prevent the fur on the ears from slipping in the case of animals such as fox, coyote, raccoon, etc., where the ears are small, and it is not practical to skin out the cartilage. **Before** such skins are put in the tan, take a steel comb and pound the teeth through the ear on both sides. If you do not have a steel comb, use a needle. Do this until the entire surface of the ears is punctured with many holes. Then rub in salt on both sides. These directions apply only to fresh hides. If the ears are dried it will not do any good.

Removing the Heads

If you are tanning hides for **robes,** you will probably not wish the heads on, hence they should be cut off and saved for other purposes. You can also cut off the feet. Simply tan the body skin.

If, however, you are tanning the hides for **rugs,** you will of course wish the heads on the rugs and you should proceed as follows:

Cut the heads off from the skin at the neck and tan only the body skin as directed in this lesson. Take the head after shaving it down and skinning out the ears and place the scalp in the **pickle-bath,** which is fully described in another lesson. When you are ready to make the rug you mount the head skin and sew it onto the body skin. Some Taxidermists tan the head skin with the body, but probably it will be a little easier for the beginner to remove the head. In order to mount the head well you must have the skin thoroughly pickled so it can be stretched to its natural size. Further information on this subject is taken up under the subject of Rug Making.

GENERAL INSTRUCTIONS

If you will carefully follow our instructions you will find you can turn out good tanning after a little experience. If after tanning, oiling and thoroughly tubbing the hide it is not soft and pliable, look for one of these causes:

1—Unprime (summer) hide. These must be left thicker than prime hides to avoid cutting roots of the hair. The only remedy is continued tubbing.

2—It is possible to wash a hide too thoroughly after the tan so that the tanning chemicals are all removed. This is indicated by black spots on the hide and must be guarded against.

3—The hide was not properly shaved down.

4—The hide has not been thoroughly oiled and tubbed.

Important—When preparing hides such as **lynx, wild cat** and others that have **soft fur,** you should not soak them in water, for if you do the fur is apt to get in bad condition and you cannot straighten it out again. Therefore when relaxing dry skins of this kind, it is best to **bury them in wet sawdust.** Then take them out and shave them down occasionally and put them back in wet sawdust and continue to do this until you have the **hide soft and pliable.** You can then proceed to tan them the same as you do hides that have been soaked in water.

For hides that are thick and heavy you can use **more acid** than for hides that are thin and flimsy. Keep this in mind when you are making up your tanning solution.

After you have tanned a few hides of various sizes, your judgment will tell you just exactly how to mix the tanning liquor, so that it will do best work under all conditions. We have given you a formula that is **satisfactory** in every detail, and it now remains for you to perform the **actual work,** which you will find very interesting. It is not play by any means to properly handle and tan heavy hides; on the other hand, it takes good honest work—but then this is required in anything we do well.

SECOND METHOD

Applicable to all skins and furs.

Wash hair thoroughly with rain water, if obtainable, and good soap. Rinse in clean water and squeeze until most of the water is removed. Remove all clinging flesh by scaping the whole interior with a dull knife. Now make a paste as follows:

Borax, 1 oz.; common salt, ½ lb.; powdered alum, ¼ lb.

Dissolve in hot water and while still hot mix into the solution corn meal, wheat flour, or rye meal until a thick paste is formed. Wipe the skin dry and apply a thick coat of the paste on the interior with a brush. Fold the skin and lay away in a dry place for 8 to 12 hours. Now unfold the skin and scrape away the paste. Wash the skin thoroughly in clean water and allow it to dry in the shade. After it becomes dry, work it over a beam and stretch with the hands until perfectly soft. With larger skins give it a second application of paste after the first has been washed away, and allow it to lie six hours longer. In tanning heavy hides, such as cow, bear, etc., several days instead of 8 to 12 hours would be necessary.

If the flesh side is all white, it is tanned. If there are spots that are not tanned, the work is unfinished. Apply the mixture of neatsfoot oil and soap suds as described under the heading "Oiling the Hides" given in the "First Method," in tanning skins with thick leather.

A chief element in all tanning is the working and manipulating of the skin after dry to break up the hardened tissue.

THIRD METHOD

Especially for fine furs.

Soak for several hours in tepid rain water. Remove and wring dry. Apply following mixture to all parts of the interior with a small brush:

Borax, 1 lb.; sulphate of soda, 1½ lbs.; saltpetre, 1½ lbs. Mix with sufficient water to form a paste.

Fold the skin and leave it for two days. Wash the interior free from paste, dry with clean towels and apply the following:

2 oz. sal soda, 1 oz. borax, 4 oz. white soap; dissolve in boiling water.

Allow the skin to lie several hours, after which it is again thoroughly cleansed.

Now immerse in a solution of 15 oz. salt, 3 oz. saleratus, 6 oz. alum; dissolve in 3 gals. rain water; allow to remain several hours.

Hang in the shade to dry, and then again place it in the solution for several hours, after which it is dried and the inside gone over with sandpaper and pumice stone. This is a most excellent method, and can be used with splendid success on the pelts of beavers, mink, otter, etc.

SPECIAL METHOD FOR SHEEP SKINS

Cut away all useless parts, soak for a few hours in water and then flesh the skins thoroughly.

For each skin mix the following ingredients to a paste with a little water, and then add just enough water to dissolve:

Borax, ½ oz.; saltpetre, ½ oz.; Glauber salts, ½ oz.

Spread this over the flesh side of the skins with a good stiff brush, applying more freely on the thicker portions.

Fold the skin with wool outside and leave for twenty-four hours.

Then wash each skin clean and apply in same manner mixture of borax or sal soda ½ oz., hard soap 2 oz., melted together.

Fold the skin wool side out for 24 hours, keep in warm place. Dissolve alum 4 oz., salt 8 oz., soda 2 oz., in enough hot water to saturate each skin, when cooled so hand can be borne in it, put in skins and leave 24 hours and then wring out and hang up to dry. When nearly dry commence to work them, and this must continue until dry and soft. Finish with sandpaper.

METHOD FOR BLEACHING WOOL

Wash tanned skins thoroughly in strong warm soap suds, rinse in clear water.

Mix Chloride Lime 4½ lbs., water 20 qts., stir until dissolved. Allow to stand until settled. Draw the clear liquor off into a solution of 10½ qts. water in which has been dissolved 5½ lbs. Glauber salts. A precipitation results which leaves a clear liquor, which is then drawn off and the skins immersed therein until they are thoroughly bleached, which takes about two days.

When sufficiently bleached, the skins should be washed first in clear water, then in a solution of good white soap to give necessary soft feeling.

SOFTENING TANNED HIDES

It is usually difficult to soften a hide after it has been tanned and allowed to dry. You should therefore use every care that the hide is properly tanned in the first place, so that it will dry soft and pliable. Also remember that there is much more to be gained from actual experience in tanning than from all the printed instructions you might receive.

A hide will dry out stiff if (1) it is not fleshed down sufficiently, (2) if the tanning solution has not been properly made, or (3) if the hide is not properly broken up over a beam. Therefore be sure to perform these three operations exactly according to instructions. If, however, the hide is still hard, place it into a weak salt-water solution until the skin is soft again. Then wash it thoroughly in fresh water and break the hide up further, as described in the lessons, over a beam. As the hide dries, pull and work it in all directions and the result should be satisfactory. An application of neatsfoot oil is also helpful.

TANNING RABBIT SKINS

If the skin has been dried, soak it in a weak salt water solution until thoroughly softened. Then flesh the hide THOROUGHLY, removing the thin layer of membrane right next to the skin. Mix together a compound of two-thirds alum and one-third salt and sprinkle this mixture lightly and evenly all over the skin side, applying it more heavily to the harder or thicker spots. Then fold the skin through the center and lay it away for about three days, turning the skin over each day. Next hang the skin up and allow the accumulated moisture to drain off, after which you should "break up" the hide by working it over a beam. This is done by drawing the flesh side back and forth over a dull edge until it is soft. (A dull knife blade, fastened to the edge of a table with the blade side up, makes a good fleshing beam.) Then mix together one-third each of mullen oil, pale paraffine oil and soluble suburban oil and apply this to the skin. The skin should then be thoroughly tanned. If still a little stiff, it can be again soak in weak salt water and worked over the beam.

Mullen oil can be secured from us at 30c a pound or if you need it in large quantities you may write direct to the National Oil Products Co.,

111 W. Washington Street, Chicago, Ill. Pale paraffine and the soluble suburban oil are both handled by any large oil company, such as the Standard Oil Co., and are now selling at about 70c per gallon. We can supply a proper mixture of the three oils ready to use at 75c per quart.

ANOTHER METHOD OF TANNING SHEEP HIDES

In such hides as this BE SURE THE HIDE IS FLESHED DOWN THINLY ENOUGH. Soak it in salt water as described above, and again flesh it down if necessary. Then wash the wool thoroughly with gasoline and sawdust or even immerse the hide directly into the gasoline. Allow the skin to drain and then mix a solution made up of 8 quarts of salt, one part of sulphuric acid and 25 parts of water. Place the skin into this formula over night and then allow it to dry thoroughly. Again dampen the skin with salt water and apply the salt and alum as described above (see "Tanning Rabbit Skins") being sure to turn the skin every day. Then apply the oil and before it is entirely dry, work the skin over a beam to break it up. Then buff skin down with sandpaper and the job is done.

Tanning Heavy Hides

In tanning large hides it is necessary to give them some **very careful preparation.** Always keep in mind the fact that a large part of the work in tanning is in the preparation of the skin, having it **perfectly soft and even all over.**

Heavy hides must be **shaved down until thin** with a currier's knife, and must be entirely clean of all fat and flesh. We do not use any acid in tanning heavy hides, for it does not penetrate sufficiently, but only tans the surface. You will therefore prepare a tanning bath as follows:

Into 4 gallons of water stir in **1 pound of powdered alum and ½ pound of salt.** For very heavy hides you can put in as much as 1¼ pounds of alum to each 4 gallons of water.

Place this solution in a barrel and put the skins into same. Be sure that all parts are submerged. As the tanning liquor works on the skin, it puts it into such condition that the fleshing knife will take hold, so after a hide has been in the solution a week or so it should be removed, worked over a beam, and fleshed as found necessary. Work all hard spots until the tissue is thoroughly broken up and made as soft as surrounding parts, so the tanning liquor can penetrate, which it cannot do if any part of the surface is hard and flinty.

After you have done this, apply to the interior of the hide a coat of **neatsfoot oil.** You can apply the oil quite liberally to heavy hides. It can be put on with a brush or cloth. After it has been oiled, hang it up in the shade for several days, then take it down and work it over a beam again, and continue to do this until the hide is nice and soft.

It is not practical to make harness or other kinds of leather without the necessary heavy machinery, drums, steam heat and other appliances with which large tanneries are equipped, so no attempt is made to give instructions in the tanning of hides without hair or into leather of this kind.

- - -

Making Buck Skin

It is not possible to produce as fine a grade of buck skin as if made in a regular tannery, but if you follow the instructions carefully and practice a few times, you will be able to turn out a quality of work that is very good indeed. Take the dry hide and soak it up for a day or two in water until it is perfectly soft and if necessary shave it down occasionally to soften up the hard spots. When the skin is perfectly soft, put it in a solution of **water and slaked lime.** Be sure that the lime is fully slaked, for if it is not, it will **burn** the skin. Use about 1 pint of the slaked lime to each gallon of water, and make it sufficient to entirely cover the skin. Now put the skin into this solution and churn it up and down until the liquid has reached all parts of the hide. Allow it to remain for two or three days or until all of the hair is **very loose.** You can tell by testing the hair when it should be removed. Now take the skin out, put it over a beam and **remove the hair and grain** with a fleshing knife, or a dull draw knife. It is best to use gloves when doing this work, as the lime is hard on the hands. After you have the hair and grain all scraped off the skin, you can wash the hide through several waters to remove the remaining lime. After this is done, you should place the hide in a tanning liquor made as follows:

To each gallon of water stir in ¼ **pound of salt and** ⅓ **pound of alum,** and continue to stir until it is fully dissolved. Now place the skin in this solution and be sure that all parts are covered and allow it to remain ten days or two weeks. When it has been in the tan a sufficient time, take it out and wash the hide thoroughly in clear water. You should now tack it out in the shade until it is almost dry, after which you should give it a very slight coat of neatsfoot oil. Then hang it up in the shade again until it is almost dry. Take it down, work it over a beam and beat it until it is perfectly soft.

Now place it in a tub of sawdust and proceed to tub it as instructed in another portion of the lessons. If you wish the hide to be white, put a little flour in the sawdust, or if you wish yellow buck skin it is necessary to smoke the hide over a smudge made of wet willows or something of this kind. You can smoke it until you get the desired color and then break up the stiffness in the leather. This is done by attaching a rope to the wall or a tree, about 6 feet from the ground, and attach the other end about 1 foot from the ground, leaving a little slack. Place the skin through this rope and pull it back and forth and you will find that it breaks up the hide excellently and makes it nice and soft. In making the tanning bath for tanning buck skin you can test it with a salinometer. It should test about 50 or 55 degrees.

HOW TO TAN HARNESS LEATHER

In order to tan shoe or harness leather, take 12 ozs. of salt, 2 ozs. of salt petre, 3 ozs. of Terra Japonica. After dissolving these in water, add 8 qts. of whey. After this has been stirred up well, add 4 ozs. of sulphuric acid. Then mix the entire solution thoroughly.

Place the skins into the liquor, working them back and forth thoroughly, strengthening the liquor from time to time when necessary.

It requires anywhere from one to fifteen days to tan the hides, depending upon the size and thickness of the skin.

When the hides are thoroughly tanned, hang them up to drain. Then oil the grain side with neatsfoot oil and hang the skins in the shade to dry. Then dip them into water so that they are damp enough to be shaved, and then shave them down well and scour thoroughly with a stiff brush. Then scrape off smoothly all the water and bits of skin with an iron sleek. Repeat this operation a couple of times on both sides of the skin.

The hide is now ready for "stuffing." This is done by making a mixture of 4 pounds of hot beef tallow, 6 quarts of tanners' oil and 2 gills of kerosene oil. When this mixture has been prepared, oil the grain side with neatsfoot oil, and again sleek out the skin thoroughly. Then brush the stuffing evenly on the flesh side, later rubbing off as much of it as possible. Then smooth down the flesh side with the fleshing knife, as smoothly as possible, and then sleek off the grain side with a stone sleek.

The coloring can be added to the leather, using any one of several leather dyes for that purpose. _____

Tanning Snake Skins

It is an exceedingly difficult matter to tan snake skins properly. It seems that the texture of the skins varies greatly, and for this reason you do not get uniform results. Therefore a little experience is the best teacher, after you understand the formulas to use.

You should tan snake skins as follows: Soak the dry skin in water until it is perfectly soft. Now make a solution of **lime and water exactly** as described for tanning buck skins. Put the snake skin in this solution and leave it two or three days. Take the skin out just as soon as the scales are loose, for otherwise it might be burned. With a stiff brush scrape the scales away, for it is impossible to tan snake skins successfully with the scales on. Now make a weak solution of alum and salt, using not more than $\frac{1}{4}$ pound of alum to each gallon of water, and about 2 ounces of salt. Place the skin in this solution and allow it to remain for a week or ten days, then take it out and wash it through several clear waters, and after this is done, hang the skin up until it is almost dry, when you should take it down and work it carefully over a beam to break up the stiffness.

You are now ready to oil the snake skin, but it is very difficult to get oil soaked into the skin, so it is necessary to apply a coat of alcohol ahead of the oil. Cover the entire surface of the snake skin with alcohol and then put on a coat of neatsfoot oil. This alcohol will soak into the skin and take the oil with it, after which the alcohol evaporates, leaving oil in the skin. After a few hours you should take the skin and work it over a beam or through a rope until it is perfectly soft.

As stated above, the results may not be entirely satisfactory until after you have practiced on a number of skins and have learned through experience just how to handle them. Snake skins, especially small ones, do not make very strong leather, and for this reason it is best to use a leather lining when making these skins into belts or hat bands. After the skins are made up it is a good plan to give them a coat of shellac on the outside. _____

Tanning Snake Skins

It is an exceedingly difficult matter to tan snake skins properly. It seems that the texture of the skins varies greatly, and for this reason you do not get uniform results. Therefore a little experience is the best teacher, after you understand the formulas to use.

You should tan snake skins as follows: Soak the dry skin in water until it is perfectly soft. Now make a solution of **lime and water exactly** as described for tanning buck skins. Put the snake skin in this solution and leave it two or three days. Take the skin out just as soon as the scales are loose, for otherwise it might be burned. With a stiff brush scrape the scales away, for it is impossible to tan snake skins successfully with the scales on. Now make a weak solution of alum and salt, using not more than $\frac{1}{4}$ pound of alum to each gallon of water, and about 2 ounces of salt. Place the skin in this solution and allow it to remain for a week or ten days, then take it out and wash it through several clear waters, and after this is done, hang the skin up until it is almost dry, when you should take it down and work it carefully over a beam to break up the stiffness.

You are now ready to oil the snake skin, but it is very difficult to get oil soaked into the skin, so it is necessary to apply a coat of alcohol ahead of the oil. Cover the entire surface of the snake skin with alcohol and then put on a coat of neatsfoot oil. This alcohol will soak into the skin and take the oil with it, after which the alcohol evaporates, leaving oil in the skin. After a few hours you should take the skin and work it over a beam or through a rope until it is perfectly soft.

As stated above, the results may not be entirely satisfactory until after you have practiced on a number of skins and have learned through experience just how to handle them. Snake skins, especially small ones, do not make very strong leather, and for this reason it is best to use a leather lining when making these skins into belts or hat bands. After the skins are made up it is a good plan to give them a coat of shellac on the outside.